NO-NONSENSE CRAPS

The CONSUMMATE GUIDE to WINNING AT THE CRAP TABLE

RICHARD ORLYN

Manufacturing by Malloy Incorporated/Ann Arbor, Michigan

Book Cover and Interior Design by Georgia Young
Additional Typography and Formatting by Erik Jay

LIBRARY OF CONGRESS CATALOGING-IN-PUBLICATION DATA
Orlyn, Richard
No-nonsense craps: the consummate guide to winning at the crap table
1st e.
LCCN: 2007936383
ISBN-13: 978-0-9791066-1-3
ISBN-10: 0-9791066-1-3
1. Craps (Game)   2. Gambling   I. Title
GV1303.O —— 2008
795.1'2 — dc21

RMJ Publishing
587E North Ventu Park Road, Suite 224
Newbury Park, CA 91320

" To my parents, Sander and Betty, who instilled in me
an acute enthusiasm for life and social interaction,
and to Mary Jane, Tristen and Brandon,
for their extraordinary tolerance during the journey.
It's not Pulitzer material guys, but I got it done. "

ACKNOWLEDGEMENTS

My sincerest heartfelt thanks to:

Jeanne McKenzie, my amazing sister-in-law, for planting the seed of this book's feasibility, and to her colleague, Joe Chuva.

Georgia Young, perhaps the most creative graphic design/advertising savant I have run into in my career, who gave the breath of life to my little book's cover and interior design. www.georgiayoung.com

Erik Jay, the "fixer," who tied all the loose ends together for me with such great adeptness and creativity. www.erikjay.com

Casino Knights of Oxnard, California, casino party gurus, for allowing me to use one of their tables for a "shoot." www.casinoknights.com

Dave Bolstad ("Boly"), Steve Gackle (the "Gackster") and *Robert Murray ("Toe"),* the Topsider crew, for their input, their support and their uncompromising friendship at the tables in Vegas.

This is NOT a book for anyone who does not believe in the ultimate random nature of the roll of two dice. In any given rotation of the dice around the table, there will be shooters who are hot and those who are not. This seemingly non-random pattern may last for multiple rotations of the dice around the table. If you truly believe that there is a reliable methodology available to predict the outcome of a particular shooter's fortune, this is not the book for you. There are plenty of books out there that pander to such gullible beliefs under the guise of legitimate probability theory. Most require that you engage in a lot of observation and/or in withholding/modifying your betting strategy based upon who's got the dice. But if you believe as I, and anyone else who understands probability theory does, that each roll of the dice is an independent random event unrelated to anything that has gone before, why would you waste your weekend trying to guess who's hot and who's not?

This is NOT a book for those who believe that it is possible to gain an edge on the house by systematically "setting" and "controlling" the roll of the dice to avoid the number *seven*. I personally think that technique is a wishful-thinking crock. But if you are blessed with incredible dexterity, have nothing but free time on your hands to practice for hours on end, have a hint of malfeasance in your blood, and are able to consistently hit a double bull on a regulation dart board at will, you may wish to look into it. You will find a number of books on the topic; it is quite the rage du jour. I'll cover the legality of such techniques later. But, the way I look at it, if I run into "The Arm" or any other hard-boiled veteran feigning dice control ability at the table, I'll be betting on the Pass Line and winning along with them.

This is NOT a book that will provide you with a multitude of betting strategies to pick and choose from and individually employ when the circumstances warrant. To advise a more aggressive betting strategy when the shooter is hot and a more conservative betting strategy when the shooter is cold is laughable. Gee, if I only knew when those streaks were coming! How often have you cranked up your number coverage or your betting increment on a hot roller or hot table only to have the dice suddenly go cold? Or backed off to have them suddenly catch fire?

This is NOT a book full of witty and colorful anecdotes, real or imagined, to support the advice and betting strategy I have presented herein. You will find that support on the table and in your wallet at the end of the day. That's not to say that there aren't stories; trust me, there are... and plenty of them. I'm merely assuming that if you wanted short stories, you'd have bought a book of short stories.

So what exactly IS this book?

It IS a book for the casual weekend craps player, for those of us that go into a casino not only to win, but to relax, have a cocktail, enjoy the music, ambience and the camaraderie of our friends, fellow players and casino guests. If you want to play for extended periods of time and not be a nervous wreck about it, you've come to the right place. But if you're looking for a quick, bring-the-casino-to-its-knees, never-have-to-work-again type win, you bought the wrong book. (And by the way, good luck with that... you'll need it.)

It IS a book that will provide you with a single, easy-to-learn betting strategy, not a series of strategies presented for you to ponder upon. It is not a particularly sexy or exciting strategy, unless you consider winning sexy or exciting.

It IS a book filled with conservative and unconventional, perhaps even counter-intuitive, thinking. Unlike the other more popularized craps betting techniques, you will probably not see anybody else at the table employing the betting strategy described herein (unless they have read this book as well). If you don't like being different, you can always join the march of the lemmings and employ the strategies of the other "experts." Happy trails!

It IS a book that addresses the issue of extended table time, not necessarily for the comps that the casino may offer you for such extended play (I'll address comps later...), but for the sake of the play itself. The longer that you're at a particular table, the more relaxing and pleasant the gaming experience will be. How many times have you ordered a drink and then left the table before it arrived due to a few cold shooters and a fear of further losses?

Lastly, it IS a book designed to help you win in the long-run ala Aesop's classical tortoise. When the shooter is hot, you will win like everybody else, but you will not win as much as your more aggressively betting counterparts (the hares). When the shooter is average, you will win or break even while many others at the table will lose. When the shooter is cold, you will lose less than you would expect (and certainly less than those hares that haven't already fled the table).

You should always expect, and be prepared, to lose when you gamble. The ostentatious surroundings, giant hotel towers and gaudy interiors of the casinos were not built from charitable contributions or governmental grants. Clearly, most people lose. If you ask someone how they fared on a trip to Vegas, they will often reply that they "broke even" or that they "paid for their trip." I am amused by those responses. In "gambler-speak", those responses equate to "I lost" or "I didn't even know that I lost because I commingled food, drink and entertainment expenditures with gambling stakes." (More about that later as well...) Slot players are the most amusing. They will usually tell you about the size of the jackpot that they hit, conveniently omitting the fact that they then reconveyed that jackpot money to its rightful owner: the house. The truth of the matter is that human nature considers losing an embarrassing outcome; one that is best kept to oneself. For a guy, losing may even assault one's manhood (haha). We all want to be smarter than the casino.

Craps is generally perceived as the most complex game in the house. (The correct nomenclature is the game of "craps" played at a "crap" table.) To the uninitiated who watch from the second row, it is a dizzying whirl of fast action, odds calculations and massive chip movement. Those of us who play derive a certain sense of satisfaction from that perception. When asked about our gaming preferences, we proudly proclaim our allegiance to the dice and make mental note of the listener's admiration. If only they knew how simple the game really is! And there is general agreement that, of all the casino games, the crap table offers some of the best odds of winning. It is a well known fact that one of the bets on the table (the Odds bet) actually provides a true 50/50 odds proposition, not available anywhere else in the casino. (I will address the Odds bet at great length later in this book.) That having been said, the proper expectation when you step up to a crap table is that you may very well lose during that session.

I have experimented with a lot of "systems" that promise consistent winning at craps. After three decades of play, I can report with a great deal of certainty that there is no such thing as a fool-proof system. If there were, authors of books like that would already be very rich and would have little incentive to write much less disclose the secrets of their success. And I do not believe, as some authors and wives' tales contend, that certain casinos have "banned" gifted players from their tables fearing the havoc that their "systems" might wreak upon the house. From what I've observed, all legal "systems" are welcome, even embraced, by a gaming industry that has time and odds on its side.

Inherent house advantages notwithstanding, I have always believed that there is the potential for optimization of session outcomes by combining a specific conservative betting strategy with money management skills that do not rely on hocus-pocus, hunches, manual dexterity, or blind luck. That strategy and those skills are about to be imparted to you.

1 | AN ODDS PRIMER

Unlike some of my colleagues, I do not intend to spend an enormous amount of time with overly tedious mathematical probability calculations. I'm going to make the grand assumption that you, the seasoned player, already know this stuff and that you, the novice, would prefer a more simplistic and straightforward approach to two-dice probability theory.

It's not rocket science. In any given roll of two dice, there are 36 possible outcomes. The first die has six possible outcomes; the second die has six possible outcomes; six times six equals 36 possible outcomes for a two-dice roll. [*See Figure 1.*]

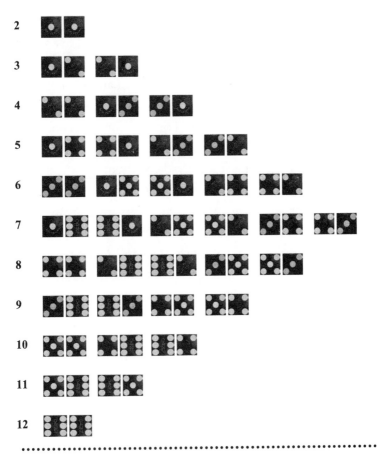

FIGURE 1: *36 Possible Combinations of 2 Dice*

The most probable outcome of a two-dice roll is the number *seven*. There are six ways to make a *seven*: 1-6, 6-1, 2-5, 5-2, 3-4 and 4-3. Thus, with 36 possible outcomes of a two-dice roll and six ways to make a *seven*, the odds of a *seven* coming up on any given roll are 6 in 36 (or 1 in 6). The fact that a *seven* is more likely to be rolled than any other number forms the basic tenet of the game of craps.

The next most probable outcomes of a two-dice roll are the numbers *six* and *eight* (referred to herein as "first tier points"). There are five ways each to make either a *six* or an *eight*. For a *six*:

3-3, 1-5, 5-1, 2-4 and 4-2. For an *eight*: 4-4, 2-6, 6-2, 3-5 and 5-3. Thus, with 36 possible outcomes of a two-dice roll and five ways to make either a *six* or an *eight,* the odds of a *six* coming up on any given roll are 5 in 36. Similarly, the odds of an *eight* coming up on any given roll are also 5 in 36. You can extrapolate the odds for all other rolls in similar fashion. For a *five* or *nine* (referred to herein as "second tier points"), the odds of either coming up are 4 in 36. For a *four* or *ten* (referred to herein as "third tier points"), the odds of either coming up are 3 in 36. The odds of either a *three* or an *eleven* ("yo") coming up are 2 in 36. The odds of either a *two* ("snake eyes") or a *twelve* ("boxcars") coming up are 1 in 36. Cumulatively, the *two, three* and *twelve* make up the group affectionately referred to as "craps" and the cumulative probability of any one of them coming up on any given roll is 4 in 36 (or 1 in 9).

The only other bit of probability understanding that is essential for intelligent play at the crap table is what I will call "probability overlay." It involves the cumulative comparison of multiple probable outcomes. *[See Figure 2.]* For instance, it is more probable on any given roll of two dice that a *six* OR an *eight* will come up than a *seven,* 10 to 6 to be exact (five ways for the *six* added to five ways for the *eight* compared to only six ways for the *seven*). Similarly, a *seven* has an equal probability of coming up on any given roll of two dice as that of a *four* OR a *ten,* 6 to 6 to be exact (six ways for a *seven* compared to three ways for a *four* plus three ways for a *ten*). Probability overlay is also useful in grasping the math behind some winning bet pay-outs. In a perfect world, if you rolled a pair of dice 36 times, you would expect to see a *seven* appear six times and an *eight* to appear a less-likely five times. The inference of that expectation is that over an extended period of play, you would expect to see five *eights* for every six *sevens.* Thus, if you were betting $5 that an *eight* would appear before a

Six Ways To Make A *Seven*

7

As Opposed to Ten Ways To Make A *Six* OR An *Eight*

6

8

Or An Equal Six Ways To Make A *Four* OR A *Ten*

4

10

FIGURE 2: *Probability Overlay*

seven during a series of rolls, and it did, the correct pay-out for that $5 bet would be $6. You could then walk away with $11, the $6 win pay-out plus the $5 bet that you had risked. Too bad that the world of craps is far from perfect.

Try it yourself. Roll a pair of dice 36 times. Record the outcomes. Did the *seven* appear six times? Did the *eight* appear five times? Did the *twelve* appear once? Probably not. That imperfection is what makes the game so fascinating and so challenging. Theoretically, the more the dice are rolled, i.e. the longer you stay at the table, the more the cumulative outcomes of the rolls will reflect the perfect-world probabilities.

2 | BASIC CRAPS SEQUENCE

The first thing I look at before I step up to a crap table is the minimum bet amount that is posted on the table, usually to both the left and the right of the boxperson. The boxperson is the one seated behind the stacks of house chips and who serves as the game overseer and arbiter of disputes. The minimum bet displays may be removable plaques or electronic displays. Either way, the minimums on the tables will change from time to time dependent upon the day of the week, the hour of the day, the relative casino traffic, etc. I will cover minimum bets at great length later in the book and the significant impact those minimums should have on your playing strategy. The minimum bet display will probably also include table maximum bets (not an issue for most of us). And, if you're lucky, the display will include the house's policy on the amount of Odds bets allowable, normally expressed as a number and a multiplier e.g. 3x, 4x, 5x, etc. Much more on that later as well. If you don't see it posted, just ask one of the dealers.

Once you find an open spot at a table with a comfortable minimum bet, wait until there's a brief lull in the action, get one of the dealers' attention, and place the amount of money you wish to have converted into chips directly in front of you or closer to the dealer, as directed, and ask for "change only, please" so that there's no confusion about whether you're seeking chips or making a bet. Your money will be deposited into a slot at the center of the table and you will be presented with the chip equivalent of your cash. Put those chips in the rack directly in front of you. There is no rush to make your first bet; take your time.

Before I make my first bet at a table, I look for the marker buck. *[See Figure 3, next page.]* That's the little black and white disc about the size of a hockey puck with "ON" written on one side and "OFF" written on the other. The marker buck will immediately tell you where the game stands in the normal craps sequence. If the marker buck is off to the side of the table with the "OFF" facing up, the next person to throw the dice is "coming out" i.e. beginning the craps sequence. If the marker buck is positioned on one of the numbers with the "ON" facing up, there has already been a point established. The strategy that I employ, and that I recommend, always begins with a Pass Line bet on the "come-out" roll. So, if a point has already been established, I wait until the present shooter either makes the point or *sevens*-out and the marker buck is "OFF" to make my first bet.

At the beginning of a new craps sequence, the come-out

FIGURE 3: *Marker Buck*

roll, if the shooter rolls a *seven* or an *eleven*, the shooter has won, has made a pass, and the house "pays-out" all bets that were made on the Pass Line. If the come-out roll is a *two, three,* or *twelve,* the shooter loses, has not made a pass, and the house takes all of the Pass Line bets away. In either of these first two cases, the same shooter continues to throw, beginning another craps sequence with a new come-out roll. If the come-out roll is a *four, five, six, eight, nine* or *ten,* a "point" has been established, the Pass Line bets are left intact, and the marker buck is positioned on the particular point in the point box area with the "ON" facing up. The only thing that matters from this juncture forward is the rolling of the same point again or the rolling of a *seven*. All other rolls are meaningless with respect to the basic craps sequence. If the shooter rolls the specific point again before rolling a *seven,* the Pass Line bets win and are paid-out, the point has been made. On the other hand, if the shooter rolls a *seven* before rolling the specific point again, the Pass Line bets lose, the point has not been made, the dice go to the next person at the table, and the sequence begins all over again.

3 | PASS LINE BET

No bet is more heralded by virtually everyone than the Pass Line bet. With only a 1.41% house advantage, it's one of the best bets you can make at the crap table. The 1.41% advantage means that for every $100 you bet on the Pass Line, you can expect to take back only $98.59. In relative casino margins, that's actually not too bad. Given a little luck and a dose of intelligent play, it's a margin that can definitely be beaten. So what does a 1.41% house advantage really mean? It doesn't mean that after hours of Pass Line play, the probabilistic expectation is that you'll only be down 1.41%. Nope. What it means is that, with each cycling of your chip total at the table, you can expect to lose 1.41% of that total. By way of an admittedly simplistic example, if you have $200 in total chips and you're betting $25 on the Pass Line, you can expect to be down 1.41% of your total after every eight craps sequences. If you stay at the table for forty craps sequences, normally less than an hour of play, the probabilities dictate that your $200 will be whittled down to $186.30, almost a 7% loss by simply betting the Pass Line (down to $197.18 after the first cycle, $194.40 after the second, $191.66 after the third, $188.96 after the fourth and $186.30 after the fifth). Imagine how bad it gets if you are making bets with much higher house advantages! But hey, we've just gotten started; no need to despair when future opportunities abound! All you really need to file away is that with each bet you make on the Pass Line you have a 50.71% chance of losing and a 49.30% chance of winning; the spread, or house advantage, is thus 1.41%.

The Pass Line bet, should only be made BEFORE the shooter throws the come-out roll and, once the shooter has come-out, may not be moved. While the casino will gladly let you make a Pass Line bet after a come-out roll, such a bet is not recommended for reasons explained later. To make the bet, you merely place the chips you are betting on the Pass Line space in front of you. *[See Figure 4, next page.]* You needn't bet on every shooter if you choose not to do so. But you must have a Pass Line or Don't Pass bet down to roll the dice yourself (although it would be incredibly rude to bet Don't Pass on your own roll; you won't make any friends at the table that way!) As a Pass Line bettor, the come-out roll of the dice is tremendously in your favor. Remember, a *seven* or *eleven* wins (six ways to make a *seven*, two ways to make an *eleven*, a probability overlay of eight ways to win out of 36 possible combinations). There are only four ways to lose with this bet on the come-out roll by rolling any craps: a *two* (one way), a *twelve* (one way), or a *three* (two ways). So you are twice as likely to win as you are to

Figure 4: *Pass Line Bet*

lose on the come-out roll by betting on the Pass Line. The problem with this bet arises AFTER a point has been established. Any point *(4,5,6,8,9* or *10)* now has less probability of coming up again than does a *seven* (six ways). Thus, you're more likely to lose on the Pass Line bet once a point has been established no matter what the point is and, it follows that, you should only make a Pass Line bet when the shooter is coming-out. That having been said, you stand more of a chance of winning the bet with a *six* or an *eight* as a point (first tier points, five ways each) than with second or third tier points *(5,9,4* or *10)*.

A winning Pass Line bet has an even money pay-out i.e. if you bet $10 and win, you get a $10 pay-out and get to keep your $10 bet. But the cumulative probabilities of the come-out roll and any subsequent rolling after a point has been established gives the house that small edge of 1.41% on Pass Line betting referred to earlier. Bottom line: In the long haul, you won't win by betting the Pass Line alone. (And if you were to do so, you'd be bored, bored, bored!)

4 | COME BET

This is where it starts to get interesting. The Come bet is often referred to as the "game within the game." The Come bet is exactly the same as the Pass Line bet except that EVERY roll is a come-out roll, hence, the "game within the game" analogy. Come bets may be placed at any time except when the shooter is coming-out in the normal craps sequence (at which point you would make a Pass Line bet, not a Come bet). To make the Come bet, you merely place the chips you are betting in the large Come area on either side of the table. *[See Figure 5.]* The Come bet wins if a *seven* or an *eleven* is rolled. The Come bet loses if a *two, three* or *twelve* is rolled. Any other roll establishes a Come point and the bet is then moved by the closest dealer to the corresponding

FIGURE 5: *Come Bet*

numbered box in the point box area of the table. And, as with the Pass Line bet, the outcome of the Come bet that was made is now entirely a function of whether or not the shooter rolls that Come point again before rolling a *seven*. If the shooter rolls the Come point again, the Come point bet (now in the point box) wins and is paid-out. Both the pay-out and the original winning bet are moved by the closest dealer to the Come area. Be sure and pick up those chips or they may be mistaken for another Come bet. If the shooter rolls a *seven* first, the Come point bet loses. As with the Pass Line bet, the house has a 1.41% advantage on this bet. Also, a winning Come bet has an even money pay-out, a $10 bet yields a $10 pay-out.

The Come bet accelerates what some feel is the slow pace of the game based on Pass Line betting alone. It allows a bettor to receive pay-outs on multiple Come point numbers as long as the shooter avoids rolling a *seven*. By way of example, let's say that a bettor puts $10 on the Pass Line before the come-out roll and that the shooter rolls a *six*. The marker buck is moved to the *six* point box with the "ON" facing up. Now, the bettor makes a $10 Come bet in the Come area. The shooter rolls an *eleven*. The bettor is paid-out $10 for the winning Come bet while the Pass Line bet remains intact. Remember, every roll is a come-out roll for a Come bet. The bettor makes another $10 Come bet. The shooter rolls a *four* and the $10 Come bet is moved by the nearest dealer to the *four* point box in the point box area. Now the bettor has two numbers covered (the *four* Come bet point and the *six* Pass Line point). If the shooter now rolls a *seven*, both bets are lost and the dice are passed to the next player. If the shooter rolls a *four*, the bettor wins the Come point bet and is paid-out. The outcome of the Pass Line bet has still not been established. If instead of a *four*, the shooter had rolled a *six*, the Pass Line Bet would have been paid-out, the shooter would start the craps sequence over again with a come-out roll, and the Come point bet on the *four* would remain in play until the shooter either rolled a *four* or a *seven*.

As discussed previously, the beauty of the Pass Line bet, shared with the Come bet, is that on the come-out roll, the bettor has a tremendous two-to-one advantage of winning. The danger occurs once a Pass Line point or Come point has been established and the house is endowed with a serious advantage. Unfortunately, on the Pass Line and on the Come, the bettor does not get to choose the point; it is determined by the random roll of the dice. Obviously, we would all prefer our points to be *sixes* or *eights*.

The Place bet accommodates those bettors that prefer to choose their own points rather than leave it to chance with a Pass Line bet or a Come bet. A Place bet may be made at any point during the craps sequence. While Pass Line bets and Come bets may be physically positioned by players, Place bets are made by announcing your intention, placing the chips that you wish to wager somewhere well in front of you (in the Come area or wherever), and allowing the nearest dealer to correctly position your bet in front of the appropriate point box. *[See Figure 6.]* Unless you expressly instruct the dealer at the table otherwise, a Place bet will be considered "OFF", i.e. not in play, on a come-out roll. That means that if a *seven* is rolled on the come-out, you will not lose your Place bet. Conversely, if your Place point is rolled on the come-out, you will not win the bet. Like the Pass Line bet or Come bet after a point is established, the only rolls that matter once the Place bet is made are the Place point and the *seven*. If the Place point comes up first, the Place bet wins. If a *seven* comes up first, the Place bet loses. Unlike the Pass Line and Come bets, the Place bet is not an

FIGURE 6: *Place Bet*

even money pay-out. If you win a Place bet made on a *six* or an *eight*, the pay-out is 7 to 6 i.e. a $12 bet will fetch you a $14 pay-out. If you win a Place bet on a *five* or a *nine*, the pay-out is 7 to 5 i.e. a $10 bet will fetch you a $14 pay-out. If you win a Place bet on a *four* or a *ten*, the pay-out is 9 to 5 i.e. a $10 bet will fetch you an $18 pay-out. Not surprisingly, the Place bet pay-outs still give the house an advantage. In a perfect world, the pay-out on a *six* or an *eight* would be 6 to 5, not 7 to 6 (remember six ways to make a *seven*, five ways to make a *six* or an *eight*). The perfect world pay-out on a *five* or a *nine* would be 3 to 2, not 7 to 5 (six ways to make a *seven*, four ways to make a *five* or a *nine*, 6 to 4 equals 3 to 2). The perfect world pay-out on a *four* or a *ten* would be 2 to 1, not 9 to 5 (six ways to make a *seven*, three ways to make a *four* or a *ten*, 6 to 3 equals 2 to 1).

So if the Place bet pay-out is better than the Pass Line bet pay-out, why wouldn't I prefer to make only Place bets? The answer is fairly simple. The come-out roll, not a factor with a Place bet, is very advantageous for the Pass Line bettor. It is the come-out roll that provides a lower house advantage on the Pass Line bet than that on the Place bet.

Before you make a Place bet, you will want to determine a bet amount that will facilitate a full pay-out in the event of a win, then express your desire to place that amount on a particular number or numbers e.g. you might say to the dealer "I'd like to place a $12 *eight*" or "give me a $12 *eight*." The Place bet pay-out on a *six* or an *eight* being 7 to 6, requires that you bet in increments of $6, hence the $12 bet to facilitate a full pay-out of $14. Not to worry; in that the house has no denominations of chips less than $1, the dealers will coach you on correct betting increments to ensure that you get a full pay-out. Unlike the Pass Line or Come point bet, the Place bet may be taken down (or modified) by the bettor at any time. You need only tell the dealer at any time before a roll "please take my *eight* (or whatever) down" and your bet will be returned to you. This flexibility can work to your advantage if used properly and will be discussed in greater detail later. Also note that in the event you win a Place bet, the dealer will dispense the pay-out but will assume that you wish to leave the Place bet intact for subsequent rolls of the dice. So, if you wish to take a Place bet down after a win, you need to request the dealer to do so.

The house advantage for a Place bet varies as a function of the number "placed." A Place bet on either a *six* or an *eight* provides the house with a 1.52% advantage. Relatively speaking, still not too shabby. Place bets on the other points increase the house's advantage significantly, to 4.00% for the *five* or *nine*, and to 6.67% for the *four* or *ten*. This escalation in the house advantage is a function of the increasing disparity between perfect world pay-outs and the pay-outs that the house actually offers. Thus, Place bets on points other than the *six* or *eight* are not recommended.

If you play enough craps, you will see a lot of people "bet the spread" after a point has been established. In so doing, they will make individual Place bets on all box numbers (excepting the Pass Line point if they already have that covered). These bettors are hoping that the shooter has a long roll punctuated with many points being rolled before the inevitable *seven* comes up, at which point they lose all of their Place bets. The more daring of the "spread" crowd will "press" their Place bets in the event of a win, thereby increasing the amount of the Place bet on the respective number. If the shooter, in fact, has a long roll without a *seven* in sight, such a strategy can be particularly lucrative. However, more often than not, the *seven* rears its ugly head before the outlay for such a betting strategy has been recouped. Remember that, while a *six* or an *eight* Place bet carries with it only a 1.52% house advantage, the *five* or *nine* Place bet comes burdened with a 4.00% house advantage, the *four* or *ten* with a 6.67% house advantage. The more sophisticated spread bettors may try to level the playing field a bit by "buying", rather than "placing", the *four* and *ten* points, a bet covered in Chapter 8, and thereby lowering the house's advantage on those two numbers from 6.67% to a mere 4.76% (eeek!). The truth of the matter is that making Place bets on the entire spread means you pick up a weighted average of all of those house advantages and end up with a very significant composite of risk. Not recommended.

6 | ODDS BET

Now we come to the most interesting and mysterious bet on the crap table. First, unlike all other bets, there is no mention whatever of the Odds bet on the table layout, where you make it, how much it pays, etc. Second, it is the only bet in the casino for which the house has no advantage; it is truly a 50/50 proposition. Stated succinctly, Odds bets effectively increase the amount of your bet on a Pass Line point or a Come bet point but with better pay-outs in the event of a win. I used to think that the 50/50 nature of the bet was explanation enough for why casinos chose to omit it from the normal crap table bet labeling; the house was obviously trying to keep the bet inconspicuous and underplayed. I've noticed that novice players, upon discovering the nature of this "hidden" bet, feel like they have procured the long sought-after secret for dominance over the game. Further, the how-to books are resplendent with praise for the bet. Some advise that the player load up the Odds bet to the full extent that the house will allow or, in the extreme, that they actually seek out and play exclusively at casinos with the highest Odds bet limitations.

But the curious nature of the bet doesn't stop there. I have found that the dealers at the table actually promote the bet, often advising beginners and others that are not taking the Odds bet to do so, citing the "best bet in the house" reasoning. Some will even raise a disapproving eyebrow when the player chooses not to make the bet as if to say "Oh well, your loss." Even though it's not labeled, most players seem to know about the bet. Just take a look at the Pass Line; there are very few players, if any, that haven't taken the Odds bet on their Pass Line point. And if all of this weren't enough to confuse the presumed merits of the Odds bet, consider the casino rules that limit the size of these bets. The Odds bet will be limited to an amount that is some multiplier of your Pass Line or Come point bet, often to three times that amount for a *four* or *ten* point, four times that amount for a *five* or *nine* point, and five times that amount for a *six* or *eight* point. This 3x, 4x, 5x limitation criteria ostensibly simplifies pay-outs of full odds winning bets for table personnel, each win requiring total payouts that are an even 7x the original Pass Line or Come point bet. (But don't worry about the math just yet.) And while some casinos restrict the size of Odds bets, others use extremely large Odds bet limitations, as high as 100x your Pass Line or Come point bet, as a well-advertised marketing tool to draw craps players eager to make such large Odds bets. What is up with the mixed messages being sent on the Odds bet? Is it pro-player or pro-house? It is somewhat of a conundrum to me. (I promised myself that I would use that word at least once in this text.) I'll relay my final thoughts on the bet once I've discussed the mechanics involved.

The Odds bet may only be made once a point has been established, so you'll want to hold off during the come-out roll. For right bettors, those betting that the shooter will make a pass, the bet is only available for those playing the Pass Line or the Come and the correct terminology for the bet is "taking odds." In the next chapter on Wrong Betting (betting that the shooter will not make a pass), I'll cover the mirror image "laying" of odds for Don't Pass and Don't Come bettors. Assuming that you're playing the Pass Line, once the point has been established, you may take an Odds bet on that point by placing additional chips directly behind your bet on the Pass Line, outside the lined area. [See Figure 7.] Like the Place Bet, the Odds bet may be removed, decreased, increased, whatever,

FIGURE 7: *Pass Line Odds Bet*

between rolls of the dice, a nice little bit of flexibility that I'll be addressing later. Also, like the Place bet, the Odds bet should be made in increments that facilitate a full pay-out by the dealer in the event of a win. If the shooter *sevens*-out before making the point, both the Pass Line bets and the Odds bets are lost. If, on the other hand, the shooter rolls the point before a *seven*, the Pass Line bets are paid-out evenly (one to one), as discussed previously, but the Odds bet pay-out is point specific: for a *four* or *ten*, the pay-out is 2 to 1, for a *five* or *nine*, the pay-out is 3 to 2, for a *six* or *eight*, the pay-out is 6 to 5. Thus, if you are playing $5 on the Pass Line, a point has been established, and you wish to make a single Odds bet on the Pass Line point as well, you may bet an additional $5, for instance, if the point is *four, ten, six* or *eight* (facilitating a 2 to 1 or 6 to 5 pay-out, respectively). However, if the point is a *five* or a *nine*, you will want to take the Odds bet in even number increments. In this instance, your Odds bet on a *five* or *nine* point would likely be $6, just a tad over single odds.

You will note that the pay-out on the Odds bet is precisely in line with the probability of the particular point coming up in relation to a *seven*. Remember, there are six ways to make a *seven* and three ways each to make a *four* or a *ten*. If your point is a *four* or a *ten*, it is twice as likely that a *seven* will be rolled first, hence the 2 to 1 pay-out on the Odds bet if a *four* or a *ten* is rolled before a *seven*. Similarly, there are five ways each to make a *six* or an *eight*, hence the 6 to 5 pay-out on an Odds bet. That is why the Odds bet is truly a 50/50 proposition with no advantage for the house; and that is why all of the gaming pundits are so exuberant about the Odds bet, extolling its virtues over all other bets.

As previously noted, Odds bets may be made for Come points as well as for Pass Line points. For instance, if you make a $10 Come bet and the shooter rolls an *eight*, you may take the Odds bet on the *eight* by passing additional chips to the dealer and proclaiming that you wish to take "odds on the *eight*." The dealer will take your Odds bet and place it atop your Come point bet in the point box, slightly skewed to one side to distinguish it from the rest of your bet. *[See Figure 8.]* It should be noted that, like Place bets and Come point bets, Come point Odds bets remain in place on the table when the shooter makes a Pass Line point but, like the Place bet, the Come point Odds bet is "OFF" i.e. not in play on the come-out roll. To clarify this situation, if the shooter has made his or her Pass Line point and you still have a Come point bet on another number with an Odds bet, those bets remain where they are. On the shooter's next roll, a come-out roll, if the shooter rolls a *seven*, the Pass Line bets win and the Come point bets lose, but any Come point Odds bets are returned to

FIGURE 8: *Come Point Odds Bet*

you. That's because the Odds bets were "OFF" on the come-out.

So where do I end up on my assessment of the Odds bet and how do I reconcile the confusing and seemingly contradictory messages associated with the bet? Don't get me wrong; I'm a big fan of the bet. It is a component of the strategy I employ myself. But there are a few things about the bet that I find curious and suspect. First, and this may be a function of my mild cynicism involving the house's motives, when employees of a casino openly solicit a bet as being in my best interest, I am naturally skeptical. Second, the wildly diverse limits that different casinos employ on the Odds bet, lead me to believe that the amount of that bet in relation to the Pass Line or Come point bet is not really all that important to the house; that the limits placed upon this bet may actually be more of a marketing ploy than anything else, not unlike the curious omission of the bet from the table layout. Shhhh ... it's a secret "unlisted" bet and the house is so afraid of its 50/50 nature that they have to place limits on it. (haha)

Here's a little bit of mathematical trivia guaranteed to give you "brain burn." You know, that throbbing pain you get when you gulp down too much frozen margarita all at once? It is widely published that the larger your Odds bet in relation to your Pass Line bet or Come point bet, the smaller the advantage for the house. Remember that the house has a 1.41% advantage on a straight Pass Line or Come bet i.e. you stand to lose $1.41 for every $100 you bet. Making even a single Odds bet (an amount equal to your Pass Line or Come point bet), lowers the house advantage from 1.41% to .85%. A double Odds bet, twice your Pass Line or Come point bet, lowers the advantage further to .61%. A 100x Odds bet lowers the house's advantage to .02%! While all of this is true, here's the mysterious and mind-numbing part: If you are betting $10 on the Pass Line, a point is established, and you decide to take a $10 Odds bet, your expectation of winning, or at least of winning more on that craps sequence, has increased, right? Nope. Still a probabilistic EXPECTATION of your losing 14.1¢. What if you take a 100x Odds bet? Nope, still the same; an expectation of a 14.1¢ loss.

Huh? Where's the disconnect here? Why bother with an Odds bet if it doesn't increase my chance of winning or my win/loss expectation? The answer is that the Odds bet, no matter how large, will always have a break-even expectation because it's pay-out reflects true probabilistic outcomes. Thus, your win/loss expectation on an Odds bet, by itself, will always be $0. On the other hand, the expectation for your money on the Pass Line or on the Come is that you'll always be down 1.41%. It is the ratio of these two bets, an Odds bet combined with either a Pass Line or a Come point bet, when taken together, that can lower the overall house advantage. The larger the Odds bet in relation to the Pass Line or Come point bet, the larger the proportion of a 0% house advantage against the 1.41% Pass Line or Come bet advantage. Feel free to pour yourself a cocktail; I'll wait.

A collateral but significant aspect of the Odds bet that I will explore at some length in Chapter 9, BASIC BET AMOUNT, is that it effectively increases the amount of every player's total bet on a number, particularly with the rampant inflation of table minimums over the past few years. In those instances where bettors feel pressure to take the Odds bet up to a house-imposed limit, the total bet they are risking on a number may be lost in the shuffle and psychologically downplayed or ignored. After all, the Odds bet is a separate, 50/50, and relatively safe wager, right? ... NOT. Remember, the *seven* will always come up more often than any point, and when it does, the Pass Line bets, Come point bets and the Odds bets all go bye-bye together. Your loss expectation for every $100 you bet is decreased by only 80¢ if you are taking double odds, as opposed to no odds, on Pass Line points. Sure, that'll add up over time... but taking large Odds bets is not nearly as critical to winning as some authors would have you believe and a great deal less critical than the factor none of us can control... the luck of the roll. The truth is that Odds bets will attenuate both good and bad fortune.

Lastly, lest I belabor this topic any further, for one to receive the true benefit of a probabilistic, perfect world, correct pay-out, like that offered for an Odds bet, one needs to stay at the table for a sufficient amount of time for the numbers being rolled to begin to approximate their expected appearances. How long is that exactly? I have no idea. Potentially, a LONG time. But from what I have observed over the years, a string of Pass Line losses coupled with the accompanying significantly larger Odds bet losses will chase a player from the table long before those probabilities even themselves out.

Wrong betting is the term used for someone that bets against the shooter. Wrong bettors want the shooter to establish a point and then *seven*-out. They are, understandably, not very popular with the right bettors at the table, particularly with those players that believe in the projection of bad karma upon the dice. I don't particularly care whether a table I play at includes wrong bettors or not because, as I've contended *ad nauseam*, I don't believe that you can will the dice to do or not do anything. However, I confess to a certain sense of satisfaction when a wrong bettor is pounded by a hot shooter. It's easy to spot the wrong bettors. They're the ones at either end of the table where the Don't Pass and Don't Come betting areas are predominantly located. Typically, they keep their hands close to their chips, as if ready to bolt from the table at the slightest provocation. They don't make eye contact with other players. They don't celebrate when they win. Sometimes when a shooter goes cold and there's an alcohol-induced aura of belligerence at the table, they'll get verbally abused by the players that lost while they won. The dealers are careful about paying them off (unlike at the blackjack table), trying to make sure that the pay-out comes from the direction of the house money, not from the direction of the lost Pass Line bets. They usually don't last long at the table. Whether they won or lost is always difficult to ascertain. They vanish without notice; you look up and they're gone.

A Don't Pass bet, made in one of the spaces normally provided at either end of the table, can only be made BEFORE the shooter throws the come-out roll and, once the shooter has come-out, should not be moved. *[See Figure 9, next page.]* You needn't bet on every shooter if you choose not to do so. As I've mentioned previously, it would be incredibly rude and potentially dangerous (depending upon the relative sobriety of the players at the table) to bet Don't Pass on your own roll. I actually have done it on a rare occasion for fun and research purposes but ONLY at a table where there were no other players. Unlike the situation for the Pass Line bettor, the come-out roll of the dice for the Don't Pass bettor is the moment of greatest vulnerability. For a Don't Pass bettor, a *seven* or *eleven* loses (six ways to make a *seven*, two ways to make an *eleven*, a probability overlay of eight ways out of 36). There are only three ways to win with this bet on the come-out roll: with a *three* (two ways) and with either a *two* (one way) or a *twelve* (one way). You will notice that the Don't Pass area includes the word "BAR" and a symbolic dice depiction of either a *two* or a *twelve*. If the *twelve* is barred, for instance, and is rolled on the come-out roll, the bettor and house push

FIGURE 9: *Don't Pass Bet*

i.e. nobody wins. The "barring" of either the *two* or the *twelve* on the come-out roll is what gives the house its advantage with the Don't Pass bet. Thus, you are much more likely to lose than win (8 to 3) on the come-out roll by betting Don't Pass. However, after a point has been established, the Don't Pass bettor's odds of winning increase dramatically. Any point (*4, 5, 6, 8, 9* or *10*) now has less probability of coming up again than does a *seven* (six ways). Thus, you're more likely to win with a Don't Pass bet once a point has been established no matter what the point is. That having been said, you stand more of a chance of winning the bet with second or third tier points than with a *six* or an *eight* (first tier points, five ways each).

A winning Don't Pass bet has an even money pay-out i.e. if you bet $10 and win, you get a $10 pay-out. But, like the Pass Line bet, the cumulative probabilities of the come-out roll and any subsequent rolling after a point has been established, gives the house a small aggregate edge on Don't Pass betting. Now, there's another surprise! Bottom line: In the long haul, you won't win by betting the Don't Pass alone.

The Don't Come area of the table is the wrong bettor's equivalent of the Come area for the right bettor. The Don't Come areas are normally located at both ends of the table. *[See Figure 10.]* They may also be incorporated within the Don't Pass area, casino dependent. Like Come bets, Don't Come bets may be placed at any time except when the shooter is coming-out in the normal craps sequence. The Don't Come bet is exactly the same as the Don't Pass bet except that every roll is a come-out roll. The Don't Come bet wins when a *three* or either a *two* or a *twelve* is rolled (whichever is not barred). The Don't Come bet loses if a *seven* or *eleven* is rolled. Any other roll establishes a Don't Come point

FIGURE 10: *Don't Come Bet*

and the bet is moved by the nearest dealer to the corresponding number in the rear point box area of the table. And, as with the Don't Pass bet, the outcome of the Don't Come bet that was made is now entirely a function of whether or not the shooter rolls that Don't Come point again before rolling a *seven*. If the shooter rolls the Don't Come point again, the Don't Come bet (now in the point box area) loses. If the shooter rolls a *seven* first, the Don't Come bet wins and is paid-out. A winning Don't Come bet has an even money payout, a $10 bet yields a $10 pay-out.

Like Odds bets being taken by a right bettor, Odds bets may be "laid" for a Don't Pass bet or for a Don't Come point bet. This "laying" of Odds is not to be confused with the stand-alone Lay bet covered in Chapter 8. I don't know why they could not have come up with more distinct terminology to differentiate the two bets! The Odds bet may only be laid once a Don't Pass or Don't Come point has been established, so you'll want to hold off during the come-out roll. If you're playing the Don't Pass area, once the point has been established, you may lay an Odds bet against that point. You may wish to announce your intention to the nearest dealer as casino conventions on the correct placement of the bet differ. As you know, the Odds bet may be removed, decreased, increased, whatever, between rolls of the dice. For wrong bettors, the Odds bet being laid also needs to be made in increments that facilitate a full pay-out by the dealer in the event of a win. If the shooter rolls the point before a *seven*, the Don't Pass, Don't Come (if applicable) and the Odds bets associated with that point are lost. If, on the other hand, the shooter *sevens-out* before making the point, all Don't Pass and Don't Come (if applicable) bets are paid-out evenly (one to one) but the Odds bet pay-out is point specific and exactly the opposite of the Odds bet pay-outs for right bettors: for a *four* or *ten*, the pay-out is 1 to

2, for a *five* or *nine*, the payout is 2 to 3, for a *six* or *eight*, the payout is 5 to 6. Thus, if you are making a $5 Don't Pass or Don't Come bet and wish to lay the Odds bet as well once the point is established, you should lay a bet that will facilitate a full pay-out to you that is roughly the equivalent of your base bet. If the point is a *four* or a *ten*, you should lay a $10 Odds bet for a pay-out of $5, if the point is a *five* or a *nine*, you should lay a $9 Odds bet for a pay-out of $6, and if the point is a *six* or an *eight*, you should lay a $6 Odds bet for a pay-out of $5. In all of my years of playing craps, I've noticed that the laying of the Odds bet is a lot less popular with wrong bettors than taking the Odds bet is with right bettors. My guess is that people don't like to make bets where the pay-out is less than the amount at risk, irrespective of the probabilities involved.

You've probably noticed that the pay-out on the Odds bet, whether in conjunction with right betting or wrong betting, and as mentioned before, is precisely in line with the probability of the particular point coming up in relation to a *seven*; it's that "the only 50/50 proposition in the house" thing again.

I don't intend to go through an elaborate contrast of the house's respective advantage over right and wrong bettors. The house has an advantage over both, but it has a smaller advantage over the wrong bettor. Just for the record, the house has a 1.36% advantage over a Don't Pass bet or Don't Come bet with no Odds bet, as opposed to a 1.41% advantage over a Pass Line bet or Come bet with no Odds bet, a whopping .05% difference. Needless to say, it is a VERY small difference, 1/20th of 1% to be exact, or a 5¢ differential advantage for every $100 bet. You're going to drop that much change on the floor by accident!

While we're on stats, and as I've already covered, the house's advantage decreases when right bettors take increasingly disproportionate Odds bets in relation to their Pass Line or Come point bets. The same is true of wrong bettors who lay increasingly disproportionate Odds bets in relation to their Don't Pass or Don't Come point bets. Wrong bettors laying single Odds bets decrease the house advantage from 1.36% to .68%, by laying double Odds bets to .46%, and by laying 100x Odds bets to a little over .01%. Contrasted with decreasing house advantages enjoyed by right bettors taking Odds bets, however, the difference in the house's advantage over the two divergent betting techniques remains nominal.

Given the ever-so-slight advantage you attain as a wrong bettor, I have never been able to understand why anyone would choose to go that route. You will note that wrong betting techniques are not incorporated into my recommended strategy covered in Chapter 10. Wrong bettors, winning or losing, never appear to be having a great time at the table. They know that they are the recipients of the scorn of a lot of right bettors at the table. For me, I want to win, yes. But I also want to have fun, and lots of it! I don't want to secretly rejoice when a table is cold and the mood is somber. And I want to revel in a hot shooter's good fortune, not skulk away counting my losses in the middle of the party.

OTHER BETS | 8

In this chapter, I'll cover all of the other bets on the table, none of which are recommended and none of which are included as part of the strategy I employ. In every instance, the house advantage is simply too substantial, often a double digit percentage advantage (ouch!). I've never heard anybody with a reasonable familiarity of the game recommend any of them, except for the Buy bet on the *four* or *ten* or maybe as an occasional hedge bet. Most of these other bets are located in the vicinity of the center of the table except for the Field bet and the infamous Big 6 and Big 8. I've seen lots of people bet on the Field; sometimes they win in spite of themselves. But I rarely see anybody take the house up on a Big 6 or Big 8 bet. I guess the word is out that you can place a *six* or an *eight* and get a 7-6 pay-out as opposed to the even money pay-out for exactly the same bet on Big 6 and Big 8.

But it's the bets at the center of the table, the hard ways and the one roll propositions, that really confound me. For each of those bets, the pay-out is nowhere near what it should be for winning such a proposition. And yet, there's always a lot of action at the center of the table. One would expect that action to be generated primarily by novices, but often that doesn't seem to be the case. The bettors that I've seen over the years involved with center table action appear to be seasoned enough to know better. I have a theory about those people. It's very flashy to constantly toss chips (usually smaller denominations) to the stickperson for center table action while invoking some of the requisite and colorful betting slang. "C&E! $5 Horn high yo!" You gotta' love it! Center table bettors usually have other action on the table with their larger bets on the numbers just like everybody else. Also, they've usually got a rack full of chips in front of them and, thus, it's very difficult to tell whether they're winning or losing. They make for a lot of noise and a lot of activity and, frankly, a lot of fun (better them than I!). They're the envy of second row spectators who assume that they really know what they're doing. I'm guessing that, for the center table bettors, it's less about winning those bets than it is about boredom, nervous energy or out-and-out showmanship.

I've known dealers to not only encourage but to defend center table bettors. Obviously, those bets are good for the house, but it goes beyond that. For the veteran dealer who knows pay-outs like the proverbial back of the hand, shifts spent at the crap table must be mind-numbing experiences on a flat sea of fatigue. Hence, the frequent breaks and rotations for dealers and stickpersons. It may be that dealers simply welcome any diversion from the conservative and repetitive betting strategies most players employ. Heavy center table action will definitely keep them awake and busy. Perhaps center table bettors are better tippers. I don't know. Whatever the case, it is true that in the few instances when the hard ways or single roll propositions are hitting, center table bettors will be garnering more significant returns than those merely betting on the Pass Line. As one dealer put it, "they'll be coloring out [exchanging lesser chips for higher denominations] and hitting the cashier's cage while the wise guys [system players] are hitting the ATM." That may very well be true on rare occasions, but I can assure you that, over the long haul, center table bettors will lose a great deal more than they will win on those bets. Without futher ado, a brief explanation of the "Other Bets" follows.

BUY BET: Same as a Place bet except that you pay a 5% commission on winnings to the house so that you get a correct odds pay-out e.g. instead of a *six* or *eight* point paying out 7 to 6 as it does with a Place bet, you would get a true 6 to 5 pay-out (like the Odds bet pay-out). Casino dependent, the commission may be payable at the outset or only in the event of a win. Assuming a minimum casino commission of $1, the amount of the bet should have the potential for at least a $20 win pay-out allowing a 5% commission of $1. With the exception of the *four* and *ten* point, if the commission is always paid, that commission makes it a less favorable bet.. So why bother? House advantage: If the house requires the commission to always be paid - 4.76%. If the commission is only paid on a win - *four* or *ten* is 1.67%, *five* or *nine* is 2.00%, *six* or *eight* is 2.27%.

LAY BET: Also known as a "backline buy" and not to be confused with laying an Odds bet on a Don't Pass point bet or Don't Come point bet, this bet is essentially the opposite of the Buy bet whereby you pay the house a 5% commission on winnings by betting that a *seven* will come up before the chosen number. Casino dependent, the commission may be payable at the outset or only in the event of a win. Assuming a minimum commission of $1, the amount of the bet should have the potential for at least a $20 win pay-out allowing a 5% commission of $1. Although you get the true pay-out on your bet, the commission makes it undesirable. House advantage: *four* or *ten* – 2.44%, *five* or *nine* – 3.23%, *six* or *eight* – 4.00%.

BIG 6 AND BIG 8: As mentioned previously, why would anybody bet on a *six* or an *eight* being rolled before a *seven* with an even money pay-out? You can make a Place bet on a *six* or an *eight* and receive a 7 to 6 pay-out. Maybe because it's a big, flashy looking bet positioned at the corners where a passerby with no clue might wish to toss the last of his or her cash. House advantage: 9.09%.

FIELD BET: Here's a beaut. And this one seems to get a lot of action. Nothing's worse than watching someone win repeatedly with this bet and then walk away wondering what's so tough about THAT game! Aaaargh... It's a one-roll proposition that the numbers *2-3-4-9-10-11-12* will come up on the next roll, paying double money for the *two* and double or triple money for the *twelve*. What's wrong with that picture? Maybe the fact that there are 20 ways of making a *5-6-7-8* and only 16 ways of making a *2-3-4-9-10-11-12*. Why would you accept even money for that proposition? Even the double money on the *two* and *twelve* doesn't justify this lame bet. House advantage: With *twelve* at double – 5.56%, with *twelve* at triple – 2.78%.

PROPOSITION BETS: These are the bets alluded to previously that are located in the center of the table. They're all bad bets, but the action is sure fun to watch! One of the more curious features of these "center table bets" is the manner in which the pay-outs are normally expressed on the table, just a tad bit deceptive if you ask me. (Please note that minor variations may occur from casino to casino.) All of the pay-outs discussed thus far have been in terms of "something" TO "something" e.g. 6 to 5 or 3 to 2. You'll note that some of the proposition bet pay-outs may be expressed as "something" FOR "something" e.g. 5 for 1 or 10 for 1. What's the difference you ask? Substantial, says I. If you are paying off someone 6 to 5 and they bet $5, they win $6 and keep the original $5 risked. They now have $11. If, on the other hand, you are paying off someone 30 for 1 and they bet $1, they win $30 but the $1 risked goes bye-bye. So isn't 30 FOR 1 really like 29 TO 1? Yup. Now, the bets...

ANY SEVEN: This is a one-roll proposition that the next number rolled will be a *seven*. The correct pay-out would be 5 to 1, right? (30 ways not to roll a *seven* against 6 ways to roll a *seven*, 30 to 6 = 5 to 1). The house pays 5 FOR 1 i.e. 4 TO 1. You get the picture. House advantage: 16.67%! The worst bet on the table!

ANY CRAPS: Another one-roll proposition that the next number rolled will be a craps (*2,3,12*). Let's see... 32 ways not to roll a craps, 4 ways to roll a craps... the bet should pay 8 to 1, right? Nope, 8 for 1 i.e. 7 to 1. Not good. House advantage: 11.11%.

THREE: A one-roll proposition that the next number rolled will be a *three*. Should pay 17 to 1 (34 to 2) but the house normally only pays 16 for 1 i.e. 15 to 1. House advantage: 11.11%

ELEVEN: Ditto, but the number is *eleven*. House advantage: 11.11%.

TWO: A one-roll proposition that the next number rolled will be a *two*. Should pay 35 to 1 but the house normally only pays 31 for 1 i.e. 30 to 1. 'Nuff said. House advantage: 13.89%.

TWELVE: Ditto, but number is *twelve*. House advantage: 13.89%.

HORN BET: This is merely a combination of four otherwise bad bets, the Two, Three, Eleven and Twelve. You bet it in increments of four and it pays off just as if you'd made the bets individually. Here's your chance to multiply a bad bet four-fold! House advantage: 12.50%.

CRAPS-ELEVEN: Another combo bet designated by the little C&E circles at the center of the table that allows you to make two bad bets simultaneously. It's an Any Craps and Eleven bet all-in-one! House advantage: 11.11%.

HARD WAYS: All of the hard way bets are multiple roll propositions that the number bet will come up "hard" e.g. a hard *four* is a two/two, a hard *six* is a three/three, etc. BEFORE it comes up "soft" OR before a *seven* is rolled.

> **HARD FOUR:** There is only one way to roll a hard *four*. There are a total of eight ways to roll either a soft *four* or a *seven*. Thus, the correct odds pay-out should be 8 to 1. The house pays 8 for 1 i.e. 7 to 1. That's not nice. House advantage: 11.11%.

> **HARD TEN:** Ditto, but the number is *ten*. House advantage: 11.11%.

> **HARD SIX:** There is only one way to roll a hard *six*. However, there are a total of ten ways to roll either a soft *six* or a *seven*. Thus, the correct odds pay-out should be 10 to 1. The house pays 10 for 1 i.e. 9 to 1. House advantage: 9.09%.

> **HARD EIGHT:** Ditto, but the number is *eight*. House advantage: 9.09%.

So why do so many people bet the hard ways?

I n the context of the betting strategy discussed in the next three chapters, I am using the term "basic bet" to mean the amount of your standard wager on a Pass Line or Come point (including any Odds bet) as well as the approximate amount of a Place bet. Many crap shooters use the wrong criteria to determine the amount of their basic bet. Many others appear to have no criteria in place whatever! Still others modulate their basic bets as a function of "gut" instinct or some other indicia completely unrelated to random probability theory. For example, they may increase their basic bet as a function of previous losses, certain that their luck must now change. Or, as if to underscore the folly of such approaches, they may increase their bet for the opposite reason, as a function of previous wins, seeking to capitalize on the "win cycle" they have stumbled upon. Without belaboring these nonsensical methodologies further, you may have guessed that I am a proponent of a fixed basic bet during any given session at the table. A fixed betting strategy is controversial; there are plenty of dissenting voices out there that contend you cannot win with fixed betting. But a fixed basic bet will make for a more pleasant, less complex session, taking the guesswork out of the process. You can certainly modify your basic bet amount at any time, provided the modification is solely a function of your aggregate winning or losing position and your accompanying willingness to accept a lesser or greater degree of risk. However, a basic bet modification should bear no relation to the outcome of a previous craps sequence or to the expected outcome of a future craps sequence. The sad truth is that there is simply no way to predict an upcoming win or loss and, it logically follows, no way to know when to bet more or when to bet less.

As you will see in Chapter 11, **Money Management**, the determination of your basic bet amount is largely a function of the total amount of money you are willing to risk during your stay at the casino. For now, I would merely like to shed some light on a number of other factors that should be taken into account when making this determination.

The first factor in establishing your basic bet amount relates to your own personal level of comfort. As a general rule, to utilize the gaming strategy promoted herein, your basic bet amount should be at least $5 and you must be comfortable risking up to four times that amount during any given craps sequence i.e. $20. If you are willing to risk up to $40 during any given craps sequence, your basic bet amount would be $10, etc. I cannot guide you further on the amount at risk that fits within your comfort level. It is strictly a matter of personal preference.

The second factor in establishing your basic bet amount is the table minimum. The fact is that, over the last few years, crap table minimum bets have been increasing at an alarming rate. These days, with Las Vegas as my reference point, unless you go to a lesser casino, you will probably not find a table with less than a $10 minimum bet. On a busy weekend, you'll find a lot of $15 and $25 minimum tables. Most of the strip casinos have installed electronic minimum bet displays and can change them from some central location instantly. By prime time on Saturday night, you'll find $50 and $100 minimum tables. Luckily, if you get on a table with a certain minimum bet established and the minimum goes up while you're playing, you'll get "grandfathered" in at the minimum with which you started. The trick is to find a crap table where the minimum bet required is equal to or less than the basic bet that makes you comfortable. Hard way bets, proposition bets and Odds bets are excluded from casino minimum bet requirements provided you have a minimum bet elsewhere on the table. However, a line bet (Pass or Don't Pass) must be at least the table minimum irrespective of your intention to subsequently take or lay an Odds bet once a point is established. Table minimums can have a dramatic impact on those players wishing to take full advantage of the largest Odds bet allowable on line bets. For a right bettor, if a $10 minimum table allows 3x, 4x, 5x Odds bets, one would be forced to have $60 in play on a *six* or *eight* point to take full advantage of the 5x odds multiple allowed ($10 on the Pass Line and a $50 (5x) Odds bet taken on the *six* or *eight* point). For a wrong bettor at the same table, one would have $70 at risk to take full advantage of the 5x odds multiple on that *six* or *eight* point ($10 on the Don't Pass and a $60 Odds bet laid on the *six* or *eight* point, the amount required to win $50, 5x the Don't Pass bet). If you were at a casino that allowed 100x Odds bets and wished to take full advantage of that limitation as some pros advise, you would have a total wager of $101 at risk on a $1 minimum table. If having that amount of money at risk does not suit your comfort level, there may be compromises required in the multiple of the Odds bet taken or laid. As you will see, such compromise is a component of the strategy I employ. Now, let's get to it...

In this chapter, I describe a craps betting strategy that I have developed and employed over the years and have coined "Table Time Plus" ("TTP") as an indication that the potential for extended table time is but one benefit you may derive from this strategy. I include TTP as part of this text with some degree of trepidation. Critics may deride its inclusion as hypocritical for someone so adamantly denying the existence of any viable craps "system." However, the potential for such criticism notwithstanding, I have chosen to include TTP herein for those readers who desire specific instructions on a manner of play consistent with the lessons of mathematical probability presented in earlier chapters. As I see it, it's better to leave you with a single course of action that you may choose to use or not use, at your discretion, than to leave you with a multitude of confusing options or, worse, with instructions that bear no relationship to the random nature of two-dice probability theory.

TTP is depicted in *Figures 11 (next page)* and *12 (page 54)*. As you will see, the strategy integrates all of the best bets on the crap table: the Pass Line, Come, Odds and 6/8 Place bets. Try not to be put off initially by the seemingly complex nature of the strategy in these figures. It is a great deal simpler in practice than it appears to be in graphic depiction. Also, know that the methodology is verbally described in significant detail in this chapter. In the following chapter, I cover the equally important money management skills required for success at the table.

As a final disclaimer, and as I have mentioned before, there is no such thing as a perfect win-all-the-time strategy. Even if you follow my advice to the letter, you will have the inevitable losing sessions. The goal is to have more winning than losing sessions and to minimize the damage of those losing sessions.

To some, TTP may seem overly conservative and measured. Once you employ it for a while, you will note that there is significant down time i.e. periods of time when you will seemingly watch the roll of dice for long stretches without any activity on your part. This is where discipline is essential. You must fight the urge to vary from the course in the event boredom occasionally sets in. Impatience is your enemy. Do what I do: order a drink, enjoy the company of your friends and tablemates, daydream, people watch, whatever... but don't stray from the formula. Thankfully, TTP is so routine and easy to follow that it lends itself to the pursuit of those other interests while gaming.

I'm not saying that you don't need to pay attention; you do. But the slower pace of TTP will leave you relaxed and less stressed out watching your money ebb and flow.

I use the term "ebb and flow" purposefully. The combination of the house's inherent advantage and the deliberately conservative nature of TTP leads to ups and downs that can often prove frustrating and tedious. I have often spent several hours at a table to find myself even or just slightly ahead or behind. It happens... but it beats the heck out of blowing your

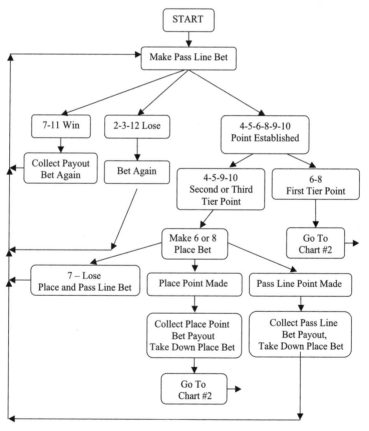

FIGURE 11: *TTP Chart #1*

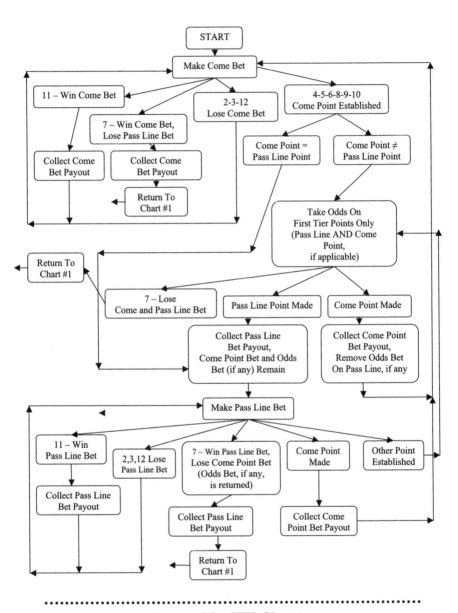

Figure 12: *TTP Chart #2*

entire stake in the first fifteen minutes at the table. The goal is to recognize the ebb and flow of the game as a natural cycle that you cannot control and to make the decision to take your winnings and walk when you are satisfied, or to cut your losses, get some rest, and wait for the next session.

I've read the advice of some that would have you believe that there are reliable disciplines available to determine the optimum time to jump in on a table. First and foremost...nonsense. Second, from what I've observed over the years, you don't always have the option of joining a game at any given instant. Often, the lower minimum tables are extremely crowded, hot or not. So do yourself a favor, discard those "timing" methodologies as more pie-in-the-sky, and get on any table at any time you want. If you find a table that appears lively and fun-loving with upbeat casino personnel and there's a spot available, go for it! Sometimes, when it's really crowded, I'll jump on an empty table all by myself. Before long, there will be others at that table too. It doesn't really matter what table you're at; dice rolls are completely random events; both good and bad sequences will come and go without warning.

TTP has two somewhat controversial fundamentals. The first is that the amount bet on a first tier Pass Line or Come point (*six* or *eight*) must be roughly twice the basic bet amount. Bets on second and third tier points must not exceed the basic bet amount. This inequity is simply a function of the expectation that first tier points will more often be winners than other points and the accompanying desire to capitalize on that expectation with larger bets. In some instances, as we will see, this will mean that you will be taking Odds bets only on *six* and *eight* points, leaving second and third tier points without Odds bets. What did he say? Blasphemy! Everybody knows that the Odds bet is the best bet in the house and should ALWAYS be taken regardless of the point, and in an amount at least double the point bet. As covered previously, taking even a single Odds bet on a Pass Line point (one that is equal to the Pass Line bet) reduces the house's advantage from 1.41% to .85%. I recognize those stats and generally advise taking Odds bets when feasible but, as I mentioned in the last chapter, there are situations related to table minimums and basic bet amounts that will require compromise on the notion of always taking Odds bets.

It is true that bettors that employ large Odds bets on all points will fare better than you will when the dice are hot. In the more predominant instances when the dice are not hot, those bettors will lose just as aggressively, and will rarely be around to reap the full benefit of the 50/50 nature of the Odds bet on very many *four* or *ten* points. Also, keep in mind that a win is a win is a win. If the shooter makes a *nine* point, you may not have an Odds bet in play, but you still win. Isn't that the point of the exercise?

The second fundamental of TTP is that you will be covering only two numbers at any given time. Will this limit your winnings when a shooter is rolling point after point? Absolutely. Will you still win during such a roll? Also, absolutely. As you probably know, there is little else in the game of craps that is more disheartening than getting good coverage on a lot of numbers just in time for the shooter to *seven*-out. The goal here is to win, of course, but also to limit losses. I am certain that you will find losing bets on two points, and only one with an Odds bet, to be a significantly less painful experience than losing three or four point coverage with full Odds bets.

For the sake of simplicity, the example that I use to describe TTP hereunder envisions a $10 minimum bet table and a corresponding basic bet amount of $10 i.e., a willingness to risk only up to $40 during any given craps sequence. In that TTP does not allow you to bet more than your basic bet on second and third tier numbers, under this scenario, you will be precluded from taking Odds bets on the *5,9,4* or *10*. There are other nuances involved with TTP, but I will cover them as we get to them. Let's get started!

Wait until the shooter is coming-out and place $10 on the Pass Line. This is the beginning of the TTP sequence as depicted at the top of *Figure 11*. If the shooter wins (a *seven* or *eleven*), take your winnings and leave the $10 basic bet on the Pass Line. If the shooter loses (a *two, three* or *twelve*), place another $10 on the Pass Line. Fairly elementary. The fun starts when a point is rolled.

It's important at this juncture that you remember the lessons of Chapter 1, **An Odds Primer**. When that all important point is rolled, we already know that no matter what that point is, there is a greater likelihood of a *seven* coming up on a subsequent roll than of that point coming up again. Thus, we want to cover one other number in addition to the Pass Line point to ensure that the number of ways for one of those two numbers to come up exceeds the number of ways for a *seven* to come up. This is where the *six* and *eight* come in. Outside of the *seven*, they are the most likely numbers to be rolled (five ways each). Thus, once a shooter has rolled a point, I want to make sure that I have the number *six* or *eight* covered as one of my two numbers. (If I've got both, so much the better!)

Here's how to do this:

First Tier Pass Line Points

If at the outset of the craps sequence, the Pass Line point established is a first tier point (a *six* or an *eight*), you would probably expect that I would advise you to immediately take an Odds bet on the point. Nope. Once a first tier Pass Line point has been established, I recommend that you immediately make a $10 Come bet without initially taking the Odds bet on the Pass Line point. There are two reasons for this strategy: First, since you already have a first tier point covered (five ways to win), you are in the enviable position of being able to let the dice choose your second number. Irrespective of that second number being a second or third tier point, you will still have a greater probability of winning by one of your two numbers being rolled than of losing with a *seven*. So there is no need to choose a specific second number by making a Place bet; let a Come point be randomly established as that number. Second, the Come bet will act as an offset to a *seven* being rolled on the very next roll, and it is amazing how often that happens. If the shooter rolls an *eleven*, your Come bet will win; take your winnings and leave a $10 Come bet for the next roll. If the shooter rolls a *two, three* or *twelve*, your Come bet will lose. Make another $10 Come bet for the next roll. If, on the other hand, the shooter immediately rolls the Pass Line point again, it is true that you will lose the benefit of having had an Odds bet on that number. But you will win on the Pass Line... and a win is a win is a win. (Note: Your Come bet, in this instance, will be moved by the nearest dealer to the corresponding *six* or *eight* in the point box area; you still have a first tier point in play!)

Once a Come point has been established, you will have your two number coverage. NOW, take a $10 Odds bet on your Pass Line point (you only had one roll of lost Odds bet opportunity). And if the Come point is the other first tier point, take a $10 Odds bet on it as well. Having two first tier points and associated Odds bets will be your moment of greatest exposure with TTP. You will have four times your basic bet at stake, in this case $40. So why only single Odds bets? Remember that, in this example, where the table minimum is $10 and my basic bet amount is $10, I have made the determination that I am not comfortable with more than $40 at risk at any given time, hence I am limited to a single Odds bet on the first tier Pass Line point and the first tier Come point bet.

If you subsequently win your Come point bet, take your Come point winnings BUT, before the very next roll, remove your $10 Odds bet on the Pass Line point and make another $10 Come bet with it. (This is actually my favorite move of TTP.) Remember, you can increase, decrease or remove your Odds bets at any time and, since this Odds bet is directly in front of you, it's easy to move to the Come area. The same two reasons discussed previously apply for taking your Pass Line Odds bet and using it to make a Come bet at this juncture. First, it will again eventually yield you second number coverage and provide more ways for the dice to deliver you a winner than a loser. Second, on the next roll, the Come bet will offset the impact of a *seven* being rolled. If the *seven* does come up and, again, it's amazing how often it will, you win the Come bet and lose the Pass Line bet, a push, rather than losing both your Pass Line bet and associated Odds bet.

If the shooter rolls your Pass Line point before your Come point, you will win your Pass Line and Odds bet but the Come point bet and Come point Odds bet that you may have on the table will remain in play. On the shooter's next roll, a come-out roll, all Come point Odds bets are automatically considered "OFF" unless you expressly instruct the dealer to the contrary. However, the Come point bet itself is in jeopardy on the come-out roll. In the event the roll is a *seven*, the Come point bet is lost and any Come point Odds bet you may have will be returned to you.

Once a new Pass Line point has been established, if you already have a Come point bet in play, remember that you've already got your two number coverage and need not take any further action.

Continue this two number coverage by making a new Come bet every time the shooter rolls your Come point and you collect your winnings. This way, you will continue to win with shooters that roll point after point for extended periods of time. And for at least the one roll when a Come point is being established, you will have a potential offset for your Pass Line bet in the event of a *seven*-out. Make no mistake, you will eventually lose; the shooter will *seven*-out. However, when that happens, you will hopefully have socked away more winnings than you will have left on the table to lose.

Second and Third Tier Pass Line Points

If, on the other hand, the Pass Line point rolled is a second or third tier point (*5,9,4* or *10*), do not take an Odds bet on the point and do not make a Come bet on the next roll. Without a *six* or an *eight* as a Pass Line point, we do not wish to leave our second point coverage to chance. Instead, use those chips to make a Place bet on the *six* or the *eight*. It doesn't matter which one, but be consistent. For instance, if the point is a *four* or a *five*, you may want to always place the *six*. If the point is a *nine* or a *ten*, you may want to always place the *eight*. Consistency in this bet will take away the guesswork and let the random nature of the probabilities work as they should. The size of the Place bet should be roughly equivalent to your basic bet of $10. So, in this case, the Place bet will be $12. Remember that for a *six* or an *eight*, the pay-out on a Place bet is 7 to 6 and you want to make a bet that accommodates a full pay-out. If you placed the *six* and it is rolled before a *seven*, the pay-out on your $12 bet will be $14.

O.K. You've got money on a second or third tier Pass Line point and you've got a Place bet on a *six* or an *eight*. Let's stand back for a second and see what you've got. Remember probability overlay? You've got six ways for the next dice roll to deliver you a loss (a *seven*). If the Pass Line point is a *four* or a *ten*, you've now got eight ways for the next dice roll to reward you with a win (three ways for the *four* or *ten* plus five ways for the *six* or *eight*). 8 to 6, not bad. And if the point is a *five* or a *nine*, you've got nine ways to win on the next roll. 9 to 6, even better.

If the shooter rolls your *six* or your *eight* (your Place bet) before a *seven*, ask the dealer to take your Place bet "down." Try and do this immediately before the dealer pays you out. Remember that dealers will normally make the assumption that you want to get paid your $14 win but that you want to leave your Place bet intact for subsequent rolls of the dice. If the dealer is annoyed by your request, remember that you have the absolute right to take your Place bet down at any time. The way I see it, you're already a $14 winner; take your winnings. However, now you're down to single number coverage i.e. the Pass Line point. We always want to be on two numbers. So, before the dice are rolled again, you should make a $10 Come bet. And from this point forward, since you've already won on this particular craps sequence, you may employ the same strategy as used with a first tier Pass Line point. If the shooter *sevens*-out on the next roll, your Come bet and Pass Line bet are a push and you still keep the $14. Granted, from this point forward in the craps sequence, you may not have the best two point coverage, but you'll always have at least the same odds of having a winner as that of having a loser. In the worst case, if the Pass Line point and the Come point are both third tier points (*four* and *ten*), your two number coverage does not give you an advantage over a *seven*. There are six ways to roll a *seven* and six ways to roll one of those third tier numbers. In these instances, I will sometimes make the only exception to the two number coverage rule and make a Place bet on either the *six* or the *eight*, just so the probability of a win still exceeds the probability of a loss. But this minor variation is up to you. You may just as easily let your two third tier number coverage remain intact. As with the first tier Pass Line point strategy, continue this two number coverage by making a new Come bet every time the shooter rolls your Come point and you collect your winnings.

There will be times with TTP when you will feel like you are standing still while everyone else is raking in the money. For instance, if the Pass Line point is *four* and you've also got a *five* Come point covered, you have no Odds bets working and only one second and one third tier point covered. The shooter could throw other points for an interminable amount of time while you are paralyzed and unable to do anything. Resist the temptation to stray; at the end of the day, you'll come out on top.

One undeniable truism of TTP is that it is first tier point, i.e. *six* and *eight*, dependent. By that, I mean that if your table goes for long periods of time with no or very few *sixes* or *eights* being rolled, the outcome will probably not be entirely favorable. The good news is that the probabilities dictate that over an extended period of time more *sixes* and *eights*, cumulatively, will be thrown than *sevens*. And if you get a streak of many *sixes* and *eights* being rolled, as often happens, you will fare exceedingly well.

In closing this chapter, I would like to step outside of the constraints imposed by my tutorial example involving a $10 minimum bet table and a $10 basic bet strategy as a means of underscoring TTP's flexibility. Let's say that your risk comfort level remains the same with a $10 basic bet strategy (you're willing to risk $40) but that you step up to a $5 minimum bet table. In this instance, you would be able to take an Odds bet on all points and still stay within your $10 basic bet profile. You would merely bet $5 (1/2 your basic bet amount) on the Pass Line (or on the Come as dictated by TTP) and take a $5 Odds bet on a *four* or *ten* point ($10 bet total), a $6 Odds bet on a *five* or *nine* point ($11 bet total, close to $10), and a $15 Odds bet on a *six* or *eight* point ($20 bet total). With a second or third tier Pass Line point, your Place bet on the *six* or *eight* would still be $12. As another example, let's say that you have determined your basic bet amount to be $25 (you're willing to risk $100) and that you are playing at a $10 minimum bet table. You could bet $10 on the Pass Line (or on the Come as dictated by TTP) and take a $15 Odds bet on a *four* or *ten* point ($25 bet total), a $20 Odds bet on a *five* or *nine* point ($30 bet total, close to $25), and a $40 Odds bet on a *six* or *eight* point ($50 bet total). With a second or third tier Pass Line point, your Place bet on the *six* or *eight* would probably be $30.

Thankfully, the experts are in general agreement that solid money management is the principal factor that separates a winning craps player from a losing one. And while there's no substitute for luck, over time, poor money management skills will catch up to you, bite you, and swallow your wallet in the process. As we've seen, TTP employs a flat betting regimen i.e. one in which the basic betting unit does not increase or decrease during a session. There are many proponents of what are termed "progressive betting systems." These systems normally require that a basic bet be increased or decreased dependent upon the outcome of the previous craps sequence or bet outcome. As you know, my fundamental problem with such betting strategies is that they fly in the face of random probability theory, suggesting that a future outcome can somehow be predicted as a function of a past outcome. That's just not the way it works, folks. There do appear to be win/lose cycles for sure, but there's no predicting when they'll begin, when they'll end, or how long they'll last. Try progressive betting systems if you must, but my advice is that you save yourself a lot of time and angst, and keep reading.

MONEY MANAGEMENT RULE #1:
Keep Track Of Your Aggregate Position

By this, I don't mean that you should have a ledger and a sharp pencil at the ready. But you do need to know where you stand in the aggregate for all of your gaming sessions. It's easy to lose track with a few bar tabs, cab fares, dinners or whatever, and even easier to estimate poorly with a heavy dose of optimism, blue sky accounting and wishful thinking. So, don't commingle your gambling stake with your spending cash! I keep a separate wallet for my stake It's easy. When you step up to the table or the cashier's cage you pull out that wallet. When you step up to the bar, you pull out your other wallet. At the end of the weekend, the undeniable truth is there in your back pocket. Just add it up.

MONEY MANAGEMENT RULE #2
Don't Be Rushed

If you have a dinner reservation in half an hour, don't step up to the crap table. You don't want to be forced to leave a table for any reason not related to the fortunes you are experiencing on the table. The good news is that TTP will provide you with some serious table time. The bad news is that TTP will require some serious table time.

MONEY MANAGEMENT RULE #3
Be Aware Of The Win/Lose Cycles

As I have written previously, craps tables seem to go through cycles, not necessarily of the same duration, but cycles nonetheless. The nature of a betting strategy can radically affect the severity of the swings in these cycles for an individual bettor. By this, I mean that an overly aggressive betting strategy can attenuate a short win cycle or a short loss cycle to such an extent that a longer, more gradual cycle never gets recognized. Thankfully, TTP, as laid out in the last chapter, has a tendency to dampen the extremes, particularly the short-term extremes of win/lose cycles. There will be a lot of very gradual ups and downs, sometimes frustrating stand-offs, but rarely any seminal events. The object is to have sufficient patience and fortitude to weather the lose or break-even cycles, to wait for a win cycle, and to ride it out as long as you feel comfortable doing so.

As I've stated, the overriding goal of money management is to have more winning sessions than losing sessions and to limit the losses of such losing sessions. As you have probably already determined, I focus less on maximizing winning sessions than most. I do not believe in gluttony. You will not bring the casinos to their knees. You will not be able to quit your job. And you will probably not conclude your weekend with the purchase of a new home or car. The wins will come, but the amount of the wins will largely determine themselves.

Consider for a moment the graphic depiction presented in *Figure 13*. Let the vertical axis represent the amount of your session stake and any wins or losses. Let the horizontal axis represent the passage of time. The slightly downward-heading straight line depicts the house's inherent advantage over time, the angle of which we have already attempted to minimize with a smart betting strategy. The house correctly assumes that if a player stays at a table long enough, he or she will eventually lose.

Now let the sine wave overlaying the house advantage line represent the ebbs and flows of winning and losing dice cycles. Obviously, the ebbs and flows that occur at the table are nowhere near as regular as those depicted in the illustration. They are usually randomly longer or shorter and vary dramatically in their intensity, both upwards and downwards. Don't get overly enamored with this simplistic presentation; I'm just trying to make a theoretical point. And make no mistake; you cannot predict an upcoming winning session by standing next to the table and trying to observe the cycles. The point of the illustration is that when you step up to the table, you may be doing so at any point in a win/lose cycle. And you may or may not have an opportunity to leave that session a winner. But the goal is to catch one of the win cycles that may be presented to you and leave the table a winner

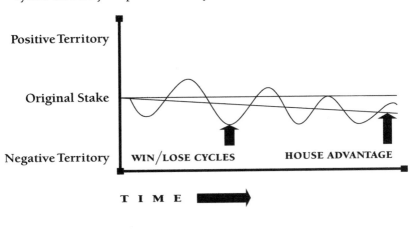

FIGURE 13: *Win/Lose Cycles Over Time*

or, alternatively, to recognize when you may not be able to battle back into positive territory, leaving the table with a minimum amount of damage. In this particular illustration, you would have been presented with two opportunities to leave the table a winner. The first two upward swings of the sine wave exceed the original stake.

This is the most nebulous bit of advice in this book and I apologize in advance for it. I certainly don't mean to suddenly go soft on my penchant for explicit instructions. But this part of money management is, by its very nature, a little "touchy-feely." Let me at least try to impart some rules of thumb for the following three scenarios: Scenario #1) You step up to a table and are up immediately and stay up. Lucky you! Scenario #2) You start down and stay down. Unlucky you! Scenario #3) You start down and battle your way back into the black.

Let's say you encounter Scenario #1, you step up to a table and begin winning immediately. When do you take your winnings and leave the table satisfied? My advice is simple; it doesn't really matter, but leave a winner. You're really lucky to have hit upon an upswing in a win/lose cycle. If you feel the cycle changing for four or five craps sequences and depending somewhat on how much you are up, by all means, take the money and run. Try and draw the distinction between a momentary downturn and a real change in the win/lose cycle. And always remember: a win is a win is a win.

Let's say you're less fortunate and begin losing immediately (Scenario #2 or #3), in my experience a very common occurrence. Don't be discouraged. The real beauty of TTP's slow, plodding nature is that, having stepped up to the table during a lose cycle, you may very well be able to battle your way back into the black (Scenario #3). Once back in the black, don't ride a cycle back into the red. Leave a winner even if the amount of the win is less than you usually take during a session. Remember the downward-heading house advantage line. You may not encounter another win cycle that gets you back in positive territory. But if, over an extended period of time, you begin to sense that you're in the midst of Scenario #2, don't be foolish. Nobody hates leaving a table a loser more than I. Hey, it happens; sometimes you have to raise the white flag; don't just immediately go to another table; go to bed; you'll get even next session.

MONEY MANAGEMENT RULE #4
Establish Aggregate Stake, Session Limit, And Basic Bet

In an attempt to redeem myself for the vague nature of the previous rule, let me provide you with some specific guidelines on effective money management. First and foremost, you need to establish the amount of your aggregate stake. I cringe at employing such an overly used cliche but your stake should equal the amount you are willing to lose during your stay. Hey, wait! The title of this book is NO-NONSENSE CRAPS: THE CONSUMMATE GUIDE TO <u>WINNING</u> AT THE CRAP TABLE. Yeah, I know. But stuff happens; I'd be foolish to promise you success every weekend. Don't include your food and entertainment budget with your gambling stake. Keep that money in a separate wallet. And whatever you do, don't break out your credit card!

Let's assume that you have decided you are willing to risk $1,500 on a particular weekend. That's your aggregate stake. The determination of your session limit and basic bet is to a large degree a function of your aggregate stake. If your aggregate stake is less, no worries. I'm only using $1,500 for the sake of example. You can impute the suggested session limit and basic bet for your aggregate stake as a fraction of the example I am presenting. (But be forewarned that if your aggregate stake is less than $400-$500, the number of sessions you can employ may be limited and you may not be able to fully apply and enjoy all of the features and benefits of TTP, even on a $5 minimum table.) Put your aggregate stake in your gaming wallet. No fudging! And when you tip the personnel at the table or a cocktail waitress with chips, it's O.K. to reimburse your gaming wallet with that amount later. The point is that at the end of the weekend, you want to know how you made out, right?

With a $1,500 aggregate stake, you can allot yourself three session limits of $500 each. That doesn't mean that you will lose all $500 of the limit in a bad session. The session limit is merely the amount of cash that you convert into chips at the table when you first step up. Never dig into your gaming wallet for additional cash during a session! The whole point of session limits is that, in the event you hit a bad session, you will have an opportunity to start fresh later. My advice would be to start considering leaving the table if you were to lose $250-$300 of the $500. Don't just immediately go to another table and start out with another $500 session. Relax, have a drink, maybe even go to bed and give it another shot in the morning. I always felt bad for my buddies that blew their entire stake the first night and ended up playing poker with each other in their hotel rooms for the remainder of the weekend. How sad is that?

Subject to the factors discussed in Chapter 9, **BASIC BET AMOUNT**, with a $500 session limit, I would advise that you start with a $10 basic bet. That amount will satisfy most of the table minimums that you will encounter for now. The general rule of thumb I use is that your basic bet be 2%-3% of your session limit, in this case, $10-$15.

So how much in winnings should you be satisfied with

before leaving a table? It's a very difficult question to answer. As I mentioned before, try to be aware of the win/lose cycles and, by all means, leave the table a winner. There is no worse sin in money management than to be considerably up, only to give it all back to the house. Don't make the mistake of considering your winnings "house money", somehow less valuable than your own. Once those chips are handed to you, it's no longer house money, it's your money, and a mere stroll to the cashier's cage away from being cash in your wallet.

With a $500 session limit, consider that a $100 win is a 20% return, a $200 win is a 40% return, etc. Quite respectable, methinks. I probably needn't tell you to ride out a winning session as long you continue to prevail. In that TTP is so deliberate in nature, it may take you a good while to accumulate winnings that you consider acceptable. I've often left a table after two hours of gaming due to sheer fatigue only to find that I was up only $25. Did I have a good time? You bet. Did I snorkel down some free drinks? Absolutamundo! And I may have scored some comp points for all of the table time. But most importantly, a win is a win is a win.

A lot of strategies I've studied suggest that you change your methodology in the middle of a winning session in order to maximize those winnings. They run the gamut from progressive betting to covering more numbers, to elaborate "let it ride" or "press" schemes. What I have found is that it's difficult enough to keep track of where you stand in any given session, much less attempt to employ some strategical derivative when the time is right. To do more than discretely count and separate my chips from time to time seems unduly burdensome. Here is my suggestion. If you find yourself in a positive aggregate position and wish to turn up the heat, with TTP you needn't change anything but the size of your basic bet. If you started at $10, go to $15 or $25. If you're really on fire, bump it even higher. Remember that increasing the size of your basic bet doesn't necessarily mean a larger bet on the Pass Line or Come but may, rather, mean adding an Odds bet or an additional increment of an Odds bet along with a larger Place bet as described at the end of the last chapter. The beauty of this approach is that it does not require additional concentration and does not speed up the pace of the game from your perspective.

That's it. It could not get much easier. Getting more aggressive on a winning weekend doesn't mean you have to stress yourself out with more complexity. Relax! Enjoy the winning sessions; they won't happen nearly often enough.

C OMPS | 12

The term "comp" is derived from the word "complimentary" and has always had a mystical connotation for me. The fact that casinos try to lure high rollers into their compound with a variety of lavish freebies is not terribly surprising. They're high rollers; they're going to get comped. For me, the real curiosity revolved around comps available to the normal weekend gambler. Everyone seems to know someone that has had a free suite for the weekend comped to them by a casino. I used to wonder whether such comps were parsed out for "excellence in losing", for the relative attractiveness of the gaming companion on one's arm, or for some other variable of a secret formula known only to pit bosses and casino management. There never seemed to be a consensus on what was required of the average gambler to receive such complimentary perquisites. My father used to walk into a casino, go to the cashier's cage, cash a $10,000 check, and walk off with the money. Back then, the casino had no good way to ascertain what my Dad did with the cash. No, he didn't gamble it away at the tables. But he did occasionally get show tickets comped to him.

Unfortunately, the mystique once associated with the allotment of comps has vanished with, among other things, the institution of casino players' cards. These are the nifty little credit card sized pieces of plastic that the casinos hand out like bubble gum to track a player's machine or table time. It is now widely understood that, unless you're a high roller, any comps received are largely a function of two variables: average bet amount and table/machine time. The casinos don't really care whether you're winning or losing at any given moment; they primarily care about the amount you're betting and the amount of time that you're at the table. And they're pretty certain that the comps will get rewarded to those that ultimately make generous donations to the house.

But my experience tells me that there are some other factors at work in the mysterious world of comps. As I've heard it said, the boxperson knows which players are providing the casino with the kind of "action" they are seeking. If you're playing a low-risk strategy with a lot of hedges and off-setting bets, it doesn't much matter to the casino how much you're betting. You're not going to win much and you're not going to lose much, thus providing the casino with no real action. I've heard these players referred to as "grinders", seemingly more interested in comps than in fiscal rewards at the table. The most hardened of table personnel may even take a disliking to such grinders, convinced that they are merely taking up space at the table that would be better suited for bona fide gamblers. I suppose that some might consider TTP a low action strategy; it is admittedly a conservative approach. However, from what I've observed, and based upon the comps I have received using TTP, the strategy is quite acceptable when combined with the most powerful and most underrated comp-getting component: COURTESY! There is no substitute for a player that is pleasant, fun to be around, and that tips his or her waitress and the table personnel on a regular basis. If you think that the table and pit personnel don't have a modicum of discretion in awarding comp credits, you're sorely mistaken.

Don't get me wrong. Although I'll normally take a player's card if it is offered to me and dutifully hand it to the boxperson every time I step up to the table, I have no illusions about my being a low priority player in the casino comp universe. In a lot of casinos, unless your basic bet is $100 or more, you're not going to glean a lot of attention from anybody no matter how courteous you are. So, ultimately, my advice is that you focus on winning at the table and don't expend a lot of energy on getting comped. If you enjoy an occasional libation, you may take solace in the comp value of an $8 - $10 call cocktail delivered to your doorstep at no charge on a regular basis. Don't order a "rum and coke"; order a "151 and coke"!

But for those that still yearn for a more substantive reward, TTP may provide you with at least one of the necessary comp components: table time. Add to that a dash of common courtesy and you may find yourself on the receiving end of comps at last!

13 │ HOUSE INTEGRITY

I get a lot of questions related to the integrity of the house. How do I know that the dice aren't loaded in their favor? After all, a die can be loaded very subtly by adding a tiny bit of mass to one side of the die so as to move the center of mass away from the geometric center. You, the recreational weekend player, would not be able to detect such subtlety. So how do you know that you're not being cheated by the house? The simplest answer is that the house doesn't need to cheat to win. The odds are that they will consistently beat you over time with straight dice. And they know that. Further, with respect to Nevada gaming, the Nevada Gaming

Commission and State Gaming Control Board keep an eye on, and regularly inspect, casino gaming and accounting practices. The stakes for the casinos are enormous. I think it extremely unlikely that a casino would risk the loss of its gaming license to gain an additional edge at the crap table. They already have an edge at that table and at every other game in the facility.

Here's the Nevada Legislature's statement of public policy from NEVADA REVISED STATUTE §463.0129.

"The continued growth and success of gaming is dependent upon public confidence and trust that gaming is conducted honestly and competitively, that the rights of the creditors of licensees [the casinos] are protected and that gaming is free from criminal and corruptive elements. Public confidence and trust can only be maintained by strict regulation of all persons, locations, practices, associations and activities related to the operation of licensed gaming establishments and the manufacture or distribution of gambling devices and equipment."

The Enforcement Division of the Gaming Control Board employs a large staff of enforcement agents that conduct regular unannounced inspections of casino surveillance systems and gaming devices including slot machines, cards and dice, and they will seize such items, if necessary. Further, there have been many independent studies conducted with casino dice, both used and new (dice are normally only used in play for a total of eight hours). None of those studies that I have reviewed have found any significant discrepancies in the entirely random nature of the gaming dice tested.

The fact of the matter is that the house is more concerned about YOU cheating THEM! Whenever a die leaves the table, you may have noticed that, once returned, it is subjected to visual scrutiny by the boxperson to ensure that someone did not substitute a player-friendly replica. Most dies are sequentially numbered to provide an additional layer of security. The boxperson (and video cameras located everywhere) discretely keep an eye on everyone at the table. Among other throwing requirements, table personnel will usually demand that the dice be thrown all the way to the end of the table hitting the far wall to ensure a random roll. And they will discourage a patron from over-handling the dice before rolling. Some lesser casinos have gone so far as to prohibit "setting" the dice i.e. positioning the dice with certain numbers facing up prior to the throw. I won't play at a casino with those kind of overly strict throwing guidelines. First, watching the wide array of shooters' throwing peculiarities is part of the fun of the game. Second, I occasionally like to "set" the dice myself, not because I can or want to control the outcome of the roll but, rather, because I enjoy seeing the point I'm hoping to make face-up before I throw. A casino that prohibits "setting" dice is playing right into the hand of those that espouse the viability of "dice control." Assuming that the shooter is actually throwing rotating dice that bounce off the far wall of the table, I am extremely skeptical of the existence of any such professed ability and categorize most of what I've read on the subject as out-and-out "fiction." Casinos that prohibit "setting" the dice probably do so more to avoid slow play than out of any fiscal concerns. I'll address dice control techniques at some length in the next chapter.

At the end of the day, if you play enough craps, you will have some uncanny sessions that defy all reasonable expectations of probabilistic outcomes. As you know by now, I'm not a purveyor of superstition. But if you are consistently experiencing losing sessions utilizing TTP (say three or four losing sessions in a row), there's no reason to play at a casino where your luck refuses to ebb and flow as it should. Go across the street and don't come back.

We all want to win at the crap table. Is there anyone among us that wishes otherwise? I think not. Some of us are so zealous about winning, that we'll make ethical concessions to achieve that end. Dice "cheats" are nothing new. Crap table personnel are trained to recognize those types. Generically, they are known as "dice mechanics", a colloquial term with dirty fingernail undertones. There is the "slider"; one who controls both dice and, after distracting table personnel, slides the dice to the other end of the table without them tumbling. Then there is the "scooter"; one who only controls one die with a similar, less detectable slide. There are a number of variations of these techniques. I've never seen any of them in action but they are the stuff of crap table lore and requisite embellishment. Most of us understand that such techniques are not legal and would no more consider using them than we would consider using counterfeit currency in a slot machine.

But what about the new generation of dice setting and dice control techniques? They're extremely popular topics with craps enthusiasts these days, spawning a virtual cottage industry of pandering books, seminars, and all other means available to separate you from your hard earned cash. In a nutshell, these theories teach that by setting the dice next to each other in a certain configuration before the roll, holding them tightly together, and flipping them together so that they both rotate next to each other around the same axis, you can take certain combinations of numbers out of play when the dice come down. For instance, if the dice are positioned with the *sixes* facing each other, both the *sixes* and the corresponding *ones* on the opposite ends of the two-dice rotating axis will be taken out of play. Hence, only four ways to make *seven* instead of the standard six ways. Skeptical? More like laughable if you ask me. Remember that you are required to have the dice hit the wall at the other end of the table to be a valid toss. Yes, that's the wall with the little pyramid-shaped rubber appendages. Good luck keeping those dice rotating on that axis! Let me know when you've got that perfected! I'm gonna' go have fun at the crap table.

It's amazing how much has been written about dice control. The internet is abuzz with the topic. Yet, with everything that is out there, I have yet to see anything that remotely resembles a statistically significant sampling of the technique's viability. And until I do, for me it shall remain fictional; a figment of an overactive storyteller's imagination; a cash cow with which to milk the gullible.

Here's a related revelation for you! Check out **§465.083** of the NEVADA REVISED STATUTE. That section states that "*it is unlawful for any person, whether he is an owner or employee of or a player in an establishment, to cheat a gambling game.*" The statute characterizes such cheating as a Class B Felony! What's that? You don't think that these vogue dice setting and control techniques constitute "*cheating*"? Really. **NRS §465.015** defines "*to cheat*" as "*to alter the elements of chance, method of selection or criteria which determine… the result of a game…*" You don't think these techniques are designed to alter the elements of chance? Really.

The truth of the matter is that craps IS a game of chance. The random nature of the game is what makes it fun, right? Why would you want to risk an embarrassing ejection from a casino (or worse) on a technique that has no merit to begin with?

You wouldn't put counterfeit currency in a slot machine, right?

Your experience, and mine, at the table will be significantly enhanced if you follow some basic rules and expectations of the house and your fellow gamers. The table personnel will occasionally be intolerant of breaches in such table courtesy. In my experience, it is not in your best interest to draw the ire of those moving your money around and accommodating your bets.

◆TIP #1: *Keep It To Yourself*

It is not your job to teach others how to play. The table

personnel will often give tips to players; that is their job, not yours. If someone at the table wants to play the "Field", "Big 6/8", or another bet that you deem imprudent, let them do so without comment. If you want to teach a friend how to play, do it in the privacy of your hotel room. Nothing is more annoying than listening to someone loudly espouse their theories of advantageous play. If asked by someone at the table about a bet, an odds calculation or whatever, give them as polite and curt a response as possible and leave it at that.

◆Tip #2: **Betting Courtesy**

The dealers (those two table personnel to the left and right of center who are responsible for moving most of the chips) normally have their hands full. Try and wait for a momentary bit of down time before thrusting your chips and betting demands their way. Keep track of where your bets are. In general, your bets will be juxtaposed in a specific betting area to coincide with your position at the table. Learn which position the dealer has designated for your bets. Picking up another players' chips is a seriously embarrassing faux pas. The dealers do make mistakes but they will be correct in their pay-outs 99.9% of the time. Be certain of your position before you engage in any pay-out dispute.

◆Tip #3: **Shooting Courtesy**

You needn't throw the dice at all if you choose not to do so. You may simply pass up your turn when it comes around. Should you choose to throw the dice, the principal house rule is that the dice reach the end of the table with sufficient velocity for them to bounce off the wall. Do your best to not repeatedly throw the dice off the table. Try not to throw the dice where they will knock over stacks of chips placed meticulously on their respective positions by the dealers. Non-shooting players should never touch the dice; don't be in the process of placing a bet just as the dice are coming your way. If you do touch the dice and the outcome is not favorable, your fellow players will be unhappy with you.

◆Tip #4: *Tolerance*

Be tolerant of the foibles and diverse skill levels of your fellow players. Don't shake your head or visibly grimace when you see someone making a bet that you consider foolish. It's their money; it's just as good as yours; and they have the right to spend it as they see fit. Shooting the dice is half the fun of the game. Everybody should get a chance to shoot. Nobody is always lucky or unlucky. As you know, I don't believe that dice roll outcomes are a function of skill. I promised no stories, but just this one. I was with a novice buddy at a table in Vegas. I was setting the dice and lofting them in a long arc to the other end of the table, not because I was seeking a non-random outcome or had any expectation of shooting glory, but because I thought it looked very cool (still do). I was experiencing a good hand, making maybe four or five passes and rolling a lot of numbers. My novice buddy had no luck shooting that night, *sevening*-out almost immediately after his point was established. A salty veteran at the other end of the table pulled me aside and told me that my friend had no business throwing the dice, that he had only made money on my rolling. What a whack job! Be tolerant.

◆Tip #5: *Tipping*

I believe in reasonable tipping as just plain good manners and civilized behavior. The people that work the tables and the waitresses that serve you don't make a great deal of money. They appreciate, and even rely on, a certain amount of tip money. I always generously tip a waitress who brings me a drink. I want her to come back soon! The waitresses gladly accept table chips for such purposes. I also tip the table personnel on a regular basis, more often when I'm winning, provided only that they've been pleasant and helpful. I'm not foolish enough to think that such tipping will somehow turn poor fortune around but I am determined to be courteous and well-liked at the table. Most players I've observed tipping will throw a chip or two into the center of the table, proudly proclaim that it's "for the boys", and then direct that the bet be placed on a hard way or other equally ill-advised proposition. My suggestion is that, if the behavior of the table staff warrants a tip, you make a Pass Line bet for them (potentially with an Odds bet, if applicable) and give your money a real opportunity to double before it becomes theirs. They always seem to enjoy that tipping method and, in my experience, are always very appreciative.

Alternatively, if you've had a cold session and have, thus, limited your normal tipping, you may simply leave a tip with the table personnel upon your departure. It's a class act in the face of a loss and will be duly noted as such by the staff.

It may be of some passing interest before closing to delve into some statistics related to casino gaming and, specifically, with respect to the game of craps and its place in the larger gaming universe. (These "nuggets" are great cocktail party fodder...)

These days, you've got a number of options with respect to practicing and playing the game of craps. Casinos are operating in over thirty states. If you reside within the borders of the fifth largest economy on the planet (California), you've got an ever-increasing plethora of Indian owned and operated casinos available to you.

However, ARTICLE IV, LEGISLATIVE, §19(E) of the CALIFORNIA STATE CONSTITUTION states that *"the Legislature has no power to authorize, and shall prohibit, casinos of the type currently operating in Nevada and New Jersey."* Thus, it was by mandate of the people that §19(F) was added allowing the Governor to enter into "compacts" with various Indian tribes that allow slot machines, lottery games, and banking and percentage card games only at casinos located on Indian reservations. A few quirky sections of the CALIFORNIA STATE PENAL CODE, TITLE 9, CHAPTER 10, §330 and 337(J) prohibit dice from being used to solely determine the outcome of the "controlled" games licensed under such compacts. Thus, "California Craps" played in Indian casinos in California, with some variations, uses two shoes of cards numbered ace through six to simulate the roll of two dice. As a side note, the California Penal Code also technically criminalizes private crap games that are "banked" i.e. players vs. the "house." Yep, in California, you can get yourself fined and/or incarcerated for playing unlicensed banked Vegas-style craps at home!

If you're less than thrilled with the "California Craps" option, or if your state of residence is not blessed with any real casino alternatives, you can always turn to in-home video game simulations or on-line internet craps gaming. On-line craps, and other internet gaming, will probably continue to experience periods of flux from time to time as a result of our elected officials' conservative legislative prerogatives. The latest assault, the UNLAWFUL INTERNET GAMBLING ENFORCEMENT ACT OF 2006 (31 U.S.C. §5361-5367), prohibits the transfer of funds from financial institutions to internet gambling sites. The capricious motives of our legislators notwithstanding, this author does not expect internet gaming, or internet craps, to go away anytime soon. For me though, neither a shoe of cards nor an animated simulation of dice rolling on a computer monitor will ever replace the invigorating chill of real dice in your hot little hand at a bona fide crap table. Call me a traditionalist, a purist, a dinosaur, whatever... I want to roll the dice!

Not surprisingly, Nevada, and most notably Las Vegas, remains the preferred destination of the North American gambling populous. As such, I have used Nevada gaming throughout this book as my basis for discussion of pertinent legislation, crap table configuration, betting and pay-out conventions.

The Center for Gaming Research at the University of Nevada, Las Vegas, reports that Vegas strip gaming revenues have increased by 376% since 1984. This increase is not merely a function of additional Vegas strip venues with casinos as one might expect (only up from 38 venues in 1984 to 40 in '06; they tear them down as fast as they build them). Rather, it is a function of larger venues, larger wagers and larger hotel capacity for the ever-increasing throngs of gambling enthusiasts. Slot machines continue to be the most popular gaming vehicle for 59% of Vegas strip gamblers; craps is claimed by a pitiful 4% of the Vegas strip flock. All the more room for us at the tables, I say! Hey, I'd be the first to sheepishly admit that the popularity of the game of craps is presently dwarfed by the other behemoths of the gaming world: Texas hold-'em, fantasy sports leagues, slot machines, etc.

So why my bullishness on craps? It's a no-brainer actually. Just walk into any casino. Who's having FUN? Slot players? Nope, a pretty sullen lot. Card players? Rarely. Serious demeanors all around. Roulette patrons? Lots of chips, few smiles. But wait... where's all that hootin' and hollerin' coming from? You guessed it, the crap table. Why would I want to be anywhere else in the casino?

The Nevada Gaming Revenue Report, produced annually by the University of Nevada, Las Vegas, tracks casino wins and win percentages for various table games and slot machines statewide. Nevada casinos took in a whopping $12.7 billion in the most recent year in which statistics are available, $8.3 billion of that from slots, the rest from table games. Interestingly and contrary to common notions, slots have a modest win percentage for the house. Casinos kept only 6.02% of money played; the sheer volume of units and massive number of players account for the huge slot revenues.

In that same year, casino craps accounted for a mere $463 million of the annual $12.7 billion in Nevada gaming revenue. But with only 408 tables statewide, that's over $1 million per table per year. Don't look at me! It wasn't MY money! Of all the table games, craps placed third in revenues for the casinos, eclipsed three-fold by twenty-one and, surprisingly, by baccarat (with only 143 tables statewide, casinos enjoy almost $6 million in winnings per baccarat table per year). The house win percentages for twenty-one and baccarat were 12.3% and 11.0%, respectively. The house win percentage for crap tables was 12.9%, i.e., Nevada casinos kept 12.9% of money played on crap tables statewide.

What do I make of all of this? How is it that, the only game in the house with an even money bet and house advantages on other bets as low as 1.41%, the casinos derive an edge on crap shooters to the tune of 12.9% of money played? I believe the answer to be twofold: 1) foolish play and 2) foolish play. Hopefully, your application of the strategies proffered herein will forever defend you from the ravages of those two afflictions.

Unfortunately, as you know, I cannot guarantee you success every time that you step up to a crap table. But I do guarantee that if you follow the advice contained between these covers, you'll have many extended, enjoyable and profitable sessions, as have I throughout the years.

With that, I wish you good fortune, no nonsense and the wisdom to discard competing dice theories not soundly based upon mathematical probability.

ACE-DEUCE: A *three* roll.

ANY CRAPS: A single roll proposition that next roll will be a *two, three* or *twelve*.

ANY SEVEN: A single roll proposition that next roll will be *seven*.

BACK LINE: Synonymous with Don't Pass Line.

BANK CRAPS: The proper name for standard casino craps where players wager against the house.

BAR: Term found in the Don't Pass and Don't Come areas along with a depiction of dice sporting a *two* or a *twelve* as an indication of which roll is a push between the house and the wrong bettor.

BIG 6 OR BIG 8: A multiple roll even money bet that either a *six* or an *eight* will be rolled before a *seven*. The bet is positioned on both corners of the table.

BOARDS: The backboard and rails constituting the raised portion around the table.

BOXCARS: A *twelve* roll.

BOX NUMBERS: The boxed areas numbered 4,5,6,8,9 and 10 used to mark the shooter's point and in which Come, Don't Come, Place, Buy and Lay bets are placed until a decision.

BOXPERSON: The casino employee seated at the center of the table who supervises the game and deposits cash in the drop box.

BUY BET: A bet made on a point number that the number will be rolled before a *seven*. The bet is paid-out with correct odds but costs the player a 5% commission, payable either at the outset or only in the event of a win, casino dependent. A coin-shaped chip designated "Buy" (a "lammer") is placed on top of the bet to distinguish it from Come point and Place bets.

C & E Bet aka Craps-Eleven Bet: A single roll proposition that next roll will be either a *two, three, twelve* (craps) or an *eleven*.

Center Table Bets: All single roll proposition and hard way wagers located in the vicinity of the center of the table.

Checks/Cheques: Chips. Most casinos use: $5 red, $25 green, $100 black, $500 purple and $1,000 yellow chips.

Choppy: Term to describe action at a table that is intermittently good and bad from a player's perspective.

Color Out/Up: Exchanging lower denomination for higher denomination chips normally before leaving a table.

Come Bet: Same as a Pass Line bet but may be made at any time other than on a come-out roll.

Come-Out Roll: The first roll of the normal craps sequence that occurs after a previous Pass Line decision.

Coming Out: A term used to describe an imminent come-out roll as in "the dice are coming out."

Comp: Short for "complimentary" and describing certain goods and services such as free rooms, show tickets, meals, etc. that the house may provide in its sole discretion as a gaming incentive to valued players.

Correct Odds: aka true odds, Odds that reflect the real world probability of a number being rolled or not being rolled, usually in comparison to a *seven*, and that carries with it no house advantage.

CRAP: The name of the gaming table e.g. "crap table" or a description of a *two, three* or *twelve* being rolled on a come-out roll i.e. "crap dice" or "crap out." Note: When a *seven* ends a craps sequence, it is correctly described as a "*seven*-out."

CRAPS: The name of the game itself or a description of the roll of a *two, three* or *twelve.*

CROUPIER: Another name for the stickperson.

DEALER: One of two casino personnel to the left and right of the boxperson charged with handling all monetary transactions and bets on their respective halves of the table.

DIME: A slang term for two $5 chips i.e. $10.

DON'T COME BET: Same as a Don't Pass bet but may be made at any time other than on a come-out roll.

DON'T PASS BET: An even money bet made immediately prior to a come-out roll that the shooter will not make a "pass." The bet loses if the shooter rolls a *seven* or *eleven*, wins if the shooter rolls either a *three* or the unbarred crap (*two* or *twelve*) and is a push if the shooter rolls the barred crap (*two* or *twelve*). Any other number rolled becomes the point, after which the bet loses if that number is rolled again before a *seven* or wins if a *seven* is rolled first.

DOUBLE ODDS: An Odds bet taken or laid that is double the amount of the Pass Line or Come bet or an amount whereby a win would equal twice the Don't Pass or Don't Come bet. Also refers to an the upper limit of the Odds bet allowed by the casino.

DOWNTOWN ODDS: Better odds afforded by some downtown Las Vegas casinos vs. Las Vegas strip casinos on certain propositions and other miscellaneous bets.

DROP BOX: A box attached to the underside of the table with a drop slot on the table layout where the boxperson inserts all cash brought into the game.

Easy Way: The numbers *four, six, eight,* or *ten* being rolled in any other way than a pair.

Edge: The house advantage/commission over a particular wager, aka spread, juice, vig or vigorish. Example: If a bet has a 55% chance of losing and a 45% chance of winning, the spread or house advantage is 10%.

Even Money: A one to one pay-out; bet $1, win $1.

Field Bet: A single roll bet that the next roll will be a *two, three, four, nine, ten, eleven* or *twelve.* Some casino layouts use the *five* in lieu of the *nine.* Of the *two* and *twelve,* normally one will pay double and the other triple. Otherwise, the Field bet is an even money bet.

Floorperson: Casino personnel located in the pit area that will supervise multiple tables.

Free Odds Bet: aka Odds bet, a bet taken or laid in conjunction with Pass Line, Don't Pass, Come or Don't Come bets, that can only be made after a point has been established and that is paid off at correct odds with no house advantage, hence "free" odds.

Front Line: Synonymous with Pass Line.

George: Dealer slang for a good tipper.

Hand: The time elapsed and passes made while one shooter holds the dice from an initial come-out to an eventual *seven*-out e.g. an "eight-pass" hand.

Hard Way Bet: A multiple roll bet that the number bet upon will be rolled as doubles, e.g. a pair of two's as a hard way *four,* before either it is rolled the easy way or before the number *seven* is rolled. Hard way bets are normally at risk (working) on a come-out roll unless the player specifies otherwise.

HEDGE BET: A bet made to offset or lessen the impact of another bet; one may win while the other loses.

HI LO BET: A single roll bet made in betting increments of two and equivalent to individual bets on the Twelve and the Two.

HI LO YO BET: A single roll bet made in betting increments of three and equivalent to individual bets on the Twelve, Two and Eleven.

HOP BET: A single roll bet that the next roll will be a specific number combination. The bet does not appear on the table layout and must be made with the boxperson.

HORN BET: A single roll proposition that combines an Any Craps and an Eleven bet and wins with a roll of a *two, three, twelve* or *eleven*. A variation of the bet, the Horn High bet, must be bet in increments of $5 and must specify which one of the four numbers is to receive the additional bet e.g. a "$5 horn high eleven" would be a $2 bet on the *eleven*, and a $1 bet on each of the other three numbers.

INSIDE/INSIDE NUMBERS: The numbers *five, six, eight* and *nine* normally in the context of a Place bet.

LAY BET AKA BACKLINE BUY: A bet made on a point number that a *seven* will be rolled before the point number. The opposite of the Buy bet and not to be confused with the "laying" of the Odds bet on a Don't Pass or Don't Come point. The bet is paid-out with correct odds but costs the player a 5% commission, payable either at the outset or only in the event of a win, casino dependent. A coin-shaped chip designated "Lay" (a "lammer") is placed on top of the bet to distinguish it from Don't Come point bets.

LINE BET: A Pass Line or Don't Pass bet.

LITTLE JOE: A *four* roll.

MARKER: An IOU from a player with credit established at the casino.

MARKER BUCK: A round plastic puck-sized disc with "ON" and "OFF" sides used to mark the point in the point box area or as an indication that there is no point established.

NATURAL: A *seven* or *eleven* thrown on the come-out roll.

NICKEL: A slang term for a $5 chip.

No Roll: A call by one of the table personnel that the roll does not count because it has bounced off the house bank, hit a player or a chip rack, or has been thrown short or otherwise run afoul of the table rules.

ODDS BET: See Free Odds Bet.

OFF: A designation that a bet is not "working", not in play, on a particular roll and potentially marked with a "lammer" stating "OFF."

OFF NUMBERS: All point numbers except for the shooter's point.

ON: A designation that a bet is "working", in play, on a particular roll and potentially marked with a "lammer" stating "ON."

OUTSIDE/OUTSIDE NUMBERS: The numbers *four, five, nine* and *ten* normally in the context of a Place bet.

PARLAY: aka Pressing or Letting It Ride, leaving your winnings in play, usually doubling your wager.

PASS: A winning outcome in a craps sequence.

PASS LINE BET: An even money bet made immediately prior to a come-out roll that the shooter will make a "pass." The bet wins if the shooter rolls a *seven* or *eleven* and loses if the shooter rolls a *two*, *three* or *twelve*. Any other number rolled becomes the point, after which the bet wins if that number is rolled again before a *seven* is rolled.

PENNY/SILVER: A slang term for a $1 chip.

PIT: The area inside a cluster of crap tables and other table games.

PIT BOSS: The supervisor of the gaming tables in the pit.

PLACE BET: A bet made on a box number that the number will be rolled before a *seven*.

POINT: Any of the numbers *four*, *five*, *six*, *eight*, *nine* or *ten* rolled on the come-out roll and which becomes the shooter's number to roll again before rolling a *seven*.

PROPOSITION BETS: aka Center Table Bets, those single roll propositions and multiple roll hard way bets located at the center of the table.

QUARTER: A slang term for a $25 chip.

RACK/RAIL: The grooved area around the top edge of the table that includes racks for players' chips.

RIGHT BETTORS: Players betting with the shooter; that the dice will pass; Pass Line and Come bettors.

SEVEN-OUT: An indication that the shooter has rolled a *seven* and has lost after establishing a point. The dice now pass to the next person at the table.

SHILL: A person employed by a casino to act as a player to start a game or to enhance the level of play at an existing game.

SHOOTER: A player shooting the dice and who has qualified to do so by making a Pass Line or Don't Pass bet.

Single Odds: An Odds bet taken or laid that is the same amount of the Pass Line or Come bet or an amount whereby a win would equal the Don't Pass or Don't Come bet.

Sleeper: A winning bet forgotten and left by a player.

Snake Eyes: A *two* roll.

Stickperson: A casino employee who controls the dice with a hooked stick, calls the number of each roll, and handles the Center Table Bets.

Table Limit: The smallest and largest bet allowed by the house at the table.

Table Odds: The largest Odds bets allowed by the house and expressed as a multiplier of the Pass Line or Come bet, or as a multiplier of the amount of a potential win on the Don't Pass or Don't Come bet.

Three Way Craps: A single roll bet made in betting increments of three and equivalent to individual bets on the Two, Three and Twelve.

Toke: A gratuity given to or placed as a bet for crap table personnel.

Working: All the bets on the table layout awaiting a decision, or an instruction from a player that his or her bets are in play on the next roll.

Wrong Bettors: Players betting against the shooter; that the dice will not pass; Don't Pass and Don't Come bettors.

Yo/Yo-leven: An *eleven* roll.